The 30-Day Productivity Plan

Break The 30 Bad Habits That Are Sabotaging Your
Time Management - One Day At A Time!

An ArtOfProductivity.com Action Guide

Damon Zahariades

Other Productivity Action Guides by Damon Zahariades

Small Habits Revolution: 10 Steps To Transforming Your Life Through The Power Of Mini Habits!

Do you have 5 minutes a day to improve your life? Adopting good habits is tough. Maintaining them is even tougher. *Small Habits Revolution* describes an unconventional, highly-effective system for forming habits that stick.

* * *

To-Do List Formula: A Stress-Free Guide To Creating To-Do Lists That Work!

Most people use to-do lists that hamper their productivity and leave them with unfinished tasks. This action guide highlights the reasons and shows you how to create effective to-do lists that guarantee you get your important work done!

* * *

The Time Chunking Method: A 10-Step Action Plan For Increasing Your Productivity

The Time Chunking Method is one of the most popular time management strategies in use today. If you struggle with getting things done, you need this action guide. Productivity experts around the world attest to the method's effectiveness!

***

The 30-Day Productivity Plan: Break The 30 Bad Habits That Are Sabotaging Your Time Management - One Day At A Time!

This action guide will help you to identify and break the bad habits that are preventing you from achieving your goals. Organized into 30 easy-to-read daily chapters, it's filled with hundreds of actionable tips.

***

Digital Detox: Unplug To Reclaim Your Life

Stress levels are rising. Relationships are suffering. Our phones and other devices are largely to blame. *Digital Detox* provides a step-by-step blueprint for people who want to take a break from technology and enjoy life unplugged.

For a complete list, please visit
http://artofproductivity.com/my-books/

Your Free Gift

I have something for you. It won't cost you a dime. It's a 40-page ebook titled "*Catapult Your Productivity! The Top 10 Habits You Must Develop To Get More Things Done.*" I'd like you to have a free copy with my thanks.

You can grab your copy by visiting the following link and joining my mailing list:

http://artofproductivity.com/free-gift/

You purchased *The 30-Day Productivity Plan* with the expectation that I would show you tips, tricks and hacks to become more productive. I appreciate your confidence in me. This is my way of saying thank you.

Contents

Foreword

The problem with most 30-day plans is that they're not designed for application. The reader is given a mountain of information organized into 30 chapters, but is left without a realistic plan for execution. That's the reason I wrote this short action guide. It's intended to fill the gap between the massive 300-page productivity books that are overwhelming to read and apply, and the information-sparse pamphlets that attempt to pass themselves off as useful aids.

This book gives you a road map toward becoming more productive. It's a true 30-day plan. It's not meant to be read and shelved. It's meant to be read, one chapter per day, and applied. It's through consistent application that you develop good habits. I've written *The 30-Day Productivity Plan* with that in mind.

Let me describe the format of the book. Being familiar with how the material is laid out will help you to put it to use.

As the title implies, there are 30 chapters. Each one is short and organized into 3 sections. The first section is a description of the problem and how it manifests itself. The second section explain how it impacts your productivity. The third section is a series of action steps designed to help you overcome the problem.

As I said, *The 30-Day Productivity Plan* is written in a way that encourages application. This isn't about theory. It's about taking action.

Is it necessary to go through the book in 30 days, 1 chapter at a time? No. You're the captain of your own ship. You decide the most efficient way to learn and use the information. You may be one of those rare savants who can skim a book and instantly recall key concepts and actionable steps. If that's the case, feel free to binge-read *The 30-Day Productivity Plan* over the next few hours. If you're like the rest of us mortals, you'll need to follow a different plan. I recommend following these four steps:

Step #1: Read through the table of contents. Familiarize yourself with the material we'll be covering over the next 30 days.

Step #2: Read *The 30-Day Productivity Plan*. Do it quickly. Don't worry about retention or application. Instead, focus on getting into a frame of mind that will allow you to absorb the material during Step #3.

Step #3: Set aside 30 days to read the book a second time. Read 1 chapter a day. Resist the temptation to progress at a faster pace. Immediately apply the action steps at the end of each chapter.

Step #4: Revisit the book every 60 days to gauge your progress. You don't have to read each chapter again. Just read the table of contents. Ask yourself how you're faring in each of the 30 areas. Conducting these quick bimonthly assessments will reveal opportunities for improvement. They'll also highlight areas in which you've made headway. Celebrate these accomplishments!

The 4-step plan above is merely a suggestion. You know yourself better than anyone. Tweak the plan according to how you absorb information. For example, you might prefer to spend a week developing each habit rather than a single day. Do so if you feel that approach will be more beneficial to you. Again, you're the captain of your ship.

The most important thing to remember is that developing productive habits takes time. It's a marathon, not a sprint. To that end, the goal is not to finish reading *The 30-Day Productivity Plan*. Rather, the goal is to use it to develop lifelong habits that help you to create and enjoy a more rewarding lifestyle.

So let's get started on our 30-day journey together!

Damon Zahariades

http://www.ArtOfProductivity.com

Day 1

Stop Checking Your Email More Than Twice A Day

According to a recent study by Statista, a statistics company, 33.9% of people in the U.S. check their email multiple times throughout the day. Just over 4% check their email 10 or more times per day while 4.8% check it 7 to 9 times per day. A much larger group (16.6%) check their email 4 to 6 times a day. Others either check between 1 and 3 times a day (39.0%) or not at all (1.6%).

The temptation to check email is understandable. Many of us need to stay updated on projects related to our jobs. Some of us pride ourselves on returning personal emails within minutes of receiving them. And some of us simply feel more engaged when we're perusing our email inboxes.

Email is seductive. It empowers us to resolve conflicts without personally confronting people. It also gives us time to manage our image and control our messaging. Email also keeps boredom at bay (but just barely). It's no wonder many of us develop the habit of checking our email over and over throughout the day.

The problem is, doing so is a productivity killer.

How This Bad Habit Hurts Your Productivity

Repeatedly checking your email harms your productivity in three ways. First, it interrupts your workflow. Each interruption forces your brain to switch tasks. Switching from one task to another - for example, from analyzing a spreadsheet to checking your inbox - slows you down. It destroys your momentum. Psychologists and researchers claim our brains need up to 25 minutes to regain our momentum after each distraction.

Second, email leaves a mental footprint. Have you ever received an email that upset you? If so, the contents probably stuck in your mind long after you closed your email software. The message distracted you from focusing on other tasks. Now, imagine how that effect can impair your ability to work if you check your email a dozen times a day.

The third way checking email over and over hurts your productivity is that it's easy to get sucked into it. How many times have you checked for new messages, an activity that should only take a few moments, only to lose an entire hour responding to people? It's like a time vacuum. It's easy to lose track of how much time you spend.

We've defined the problem and identified how it makes you less productive. Let's now take a look at several actionable tactics you can put in place to break your "email habit."

Action Steps

1. Set specific times of the day to check your email. Pick two and treat them like appointments with yourself. Test different times of the morning, afternoon and evening. Track which times best complement your schedule, energy levels and workflow.

2. Keep your email software closed while you work. If you use a cloud-based service like Gmail or Yahoo Mail, do not keep it open in a browser tab.

3. Turn off email notifications on your phone. Even if your email software is closed or your cloud-based email service is inaccessible, audible alerts that signal the arrival of new messages tempt you to check them. For many people, these notifications are irresistible. Turn them off to avoid the temptation.

4. Refrain from sending unimportant emails. The more you send, the more you'll receive. You'll also earn a reputation for being accessible via email, which will encourage others to needlessly reach out to you.

5. Tell others you only check email twice a day. Inform them regarding the times. Doing so will allow you to influence their expectations regarding when they should expect responses from you.

6. Identify the triggers that prompt you to compulsively check email. Do you do it when you're bored? Are you concerned about responding late to a potential client? Do you check for messages as a way to procrastinate on tasks? Be aware of these triggers so you can alter your response to them. (We'll talk more about triggers later.)

7. Create obstacles that make it more difficult to satisfy the triggers. For example, if you use Gmail, delete the bookmark in your browser. Or use a browser-based app like StayFocusd to block your access to the service. (Note: developing good habits is always preferable to using apps. It takes more effort, but empowers you with increased self-discipline.)

8. Develop alternative behaviors to replace the compulsion to check email. For example, if you check email as a way to procrastinate, commit to breaking that habit by working immediately on the task at hand.

Day 2

Stop Trying To Be Perfect

Perfectionism destroys relationships, hampers careers and is one of the chief causes of unhappiness and frustration. It's also a surefire productivity killer, an effect we'll talk about in more detail in a moment.

The tendency to want to be perfect stems from a variety of sources. Some of us were raised to meet others' high expectations, and have carried that anxiety with us into adulthood. In our minds, imperfection equals failure. Others have imposed upon themselves performance standards that have little to do with the benefits they enjoy from meeting them. They aim high for the sake of aiming high. Still others use perfectionism as a way to compensate for perceived deficits in other areas of their lives.

Here's the worst part: it's celebrated in our society. Kids are encouraged to study for hours on end just to achieve perfect scores on tests. Employees are pressured to turn in reports and finish projects with zero errors. Contractors are expected to deliver their services according to unrealistic deadlines.

Perfectionism is praised as an asset. Unfortunately, that encourages folks to pursue it as a goal.

Being perfect is unnecessary.

Think back to the years you spent in school. Try to recall a project for which you toiled for hours and as a result, received a perfect score. How did that A+ or 100% affect your life? If you're like most people, it had zero effect.

Think about your job. Try to recall a report you worked on for hours to ensure it was error-free when you gave it to your boss. Did your perfectionism have a major impact on your career? Probably not.

Being perfect is more than just unnecessary. It's harmful to your productivity.

How This Bad Habit Hurts Your Productivity

Perfectionism undermines your productivity in four ways. First, it prevents you from getting things done. You're so focused on completing your current task with zero errors that you rob yourself of the time needed to complete other tasks.

Second, it elevates your stress level. Studies show that individuals who pursue perfectionism are more likely to experience anxiety. You don't need me to tell you that stress and anxiety negatively affect your productivity. You know this from first-hand experience.

Third, it encourages procrastination. It's easier to continue working on a current task than to start a new one, especially if the new one requires stepping outside your comfort zone. That can easily become a bad habit, eroding your motivation to take action. You'll start to rationalize putting things off just to make sure the task you're working on is error-free.

An extension of this new procrastination habit is that you start to put off current tasks because you're concerned about handling them with perfection. You resist working on them because you fear failure. That fear is based on an unfeasible definition of success.

Fourth, perfectionism harms your self-esteem. Being perfect is impossible. No one achieves it over the long run. Striving for it is a recipe for frustration and disappointment, especially if your self-image is tied to unreasonable expectations about your performance.

If you feel as if you're failing to live up to your own standards, you'll lack the motivation to take action and get things done.

Let's now talk about things you can do, starting today, to curtail your tendency toward perfection.

Action Steps

1. Shift your focus from perfecting your work to *finishing* it. Granted, it will take time to develop and grow accustomed to this new perspective.

   Start slowly. Apply this shift in focus to a single task. With time and continued application, it will become second-nature. But expect an uphill battle getting to that point.

   Remember, you're redoing mental programming that took years to gain a foothold in your mind. Be patient with yourself.

2. Ask yourself whether the time and effort you plan to invest will help you to achieve a specific goal. For example, will spending hours perfecting that cost-analysis report for your boss result in a raise? Will studying for hours to get an A+ on next week's chemistry exam result in a solid job offer?

   Make this the litmus test.

3. Create obstacles that "short-circuit" your habit for perfectionism. For example, stand up from your desk and walk away the moment you notice yourself trying to perfect something you're working on. Alter your behavioral pattern. Take a moment to recalibrate your focus toward *completing* the task at hand rather than perfecting it. Then, return to your desk and resume your work.

4. Embrace your mistakes. Instead of criticizing yourself, use mistakes as learning opportunities. Use them to expand your knowledge, improve your work habits and become a better employee (or student, professor, musician or spouse). Practice developing and reinforcing this perspective each time you discover you've made a mistake.

5. Identify the worst possible outcome that can occur if you make a mistake. For example, if the report you're preparing for your boss contains a misspelled word, will you lose your job? If you receive a B+ on your chemistry exam, will you be placed on academic probation? Chances are, you'll survive.

Day 3

Stop Creating Overly-Ambitious To-Do Lists

If you regularly create to-do lists that are less than half completed at the end of each day, you're being too ambitious. Chances are you're filling your lists with too many tasks.

You're in good company. A lot of people make this mistake. Like them, you're making it for one of two reasons (or possibly both).

First, you're overestimating the amount of time you have during the day to get things done, or underestimating the time it will take you to do so. Both circumstances produce the same result.

Second, you're using a single list to capture every to-do item that comes to mind. Predictably, your list grows throughout the day. By the time you're ready to call it quits, you have more items on your list than you had when you began working that morning. Talk about frustrating and demoralizing!

The irony about to-do lists is that they're supposed to make us more productive. Yet, many people sabotage their productivity by creating lists that work against them. The problem has become so prevalent that many time management experts now suggest getting rid of them altogether. (I disagree for reasons that will become clear in a moment.)

How This Bad Habit Hurts Your Productivity

Overly-ambitious to-do lists erode your productivity in three ways. First, they set the stage for frustration and disappointment.

13

If you're like most people, you feel energized when you accomplish a goal and dejected when you fail. Consider that effect in light of the fact that every to-do list you create represents an implicit goal. Success is being able to cross the last item off the list. Failure is having uncompleted items on the list at the end of the day. That daily dose of frustration makes it difficult to focus and get things done.

Second, having a long list of uncompleted tasks that you're forced to carry over to the following day increases your stress. While a small amount of stress can serve as a powerful motivator, too much can quickly tip the scales, derailing your ability to work in a state of flow.

Third, if you're routinely carrying over unfinished items from day to day, you won't be able to accurately track your daily time usage. Consequently, you won't have a way to forecast how long tasks are likely to take in the days and weeks ahead.

Fortunately, with a few simple guidelines, you can start creating to-do lists that work *for* you rather than against you. Following are seven action steps you can implement today.

Action Steps

1. Get used to telling yourself (and others) "no." To-do lists grow in length because it's difficult to resist adding items to them. The act of writing them down takes only a moment, and we thus deceive ourselves about the time and effort required to complete them. Say "no" more often to keep your to-do under control.

2. Identify a compelling reason to work on every task that appears on your list. Otherwise, why would you want to devote your limited time and attention to it? Before you add a task to your list, ask yourself why you must complete it.

3. Assign a priority to every item on your to-do list. Use letters A through C. High-priority items receive an "A." Low-priority items receive a "C."

   Next, review the tasks you've assigned a "C" and ask yourself whether they're essential to your goals. If not, cross them off your list.

4. Set a limit to the number of tasks you'll allow on your list. For example, commit to never allowing your list to expand to more than five items. A short to-do list appears doable. That alone will give you the motivation you need to complete the tasks that appear on it.

5. Start with the "biggest rock" on your list. This is the task that has the highest priority. It's one of the most important things you'll do today and plays a critical role in accomplishing a specific goal. It might also be the task that's going to take the most time, introduce the most problems, and thus be the one you're looking forward to working on the least.

   Incidentally, I took the idea of "big rocks" from Leo Babauta of ZenHabits.net. I believe he took the idea from Stephen Covey. So credit where credit is due.

6. Set a reasonable time limit for each task on your list. Don't just work until it's completed. Parkinson's Law states that "work expands so as to fill the time available for its completion." If you give yourself 2 hours to finish a task, you'll take 2 hours to finish it. Give yourself 45 minutes and set a timer, and you'll likely finish it in that amount of time.

7. Use 2 lists. Limit the first list to organize your to-do items for the day. Use the second list to capture everything else that comes to mind.

Prioritize each item you add to the second list. Then, review them periodically to assess whether their priority levels need to be adjusted.

Bonus Tip

If you prefer to keep track of your to-do lists online, I highly recommend Todoist.com. It's easy to use and offers practical features that will help you to organize your day. You can create multiple lists, assign different priority levels to each task, move items between lists, set due dates and apply colorful labels for easy task management. And the best part? It's free.

Day 4

Stop Giving Yourself
Too Much Time To Complete Tasks

In yesterday's Action Steps, we noted that Parkinson's Law states that "work expands so as to fill the time available for its completion." Today, we're going to focus on this law.

Most of us give ourselves far too much time to finish tasks. Or worse, we fail to give ourselves time limits at all. We work until the task at hand is completed.

In both cases, we end up spending too much time working on things. For example, recall the last time your boss gave you a week to complete a report. You probably finished the report on the day it was due. That's not because your boss knew exactly how much time was required to finish it. It was because of Parkinson's Law. You gave yourself a week, and so the assignment took a week to complete.

In the second case (working without a time limit), we rob ourselves of a gauge with which to evaluate our progress. An hour passes and we have no clue whether we should be further along toward completing the task in front of us. It's no wonder so many tasks take longer than necessary to finish.

Working in this way negatively affects your ability to get things done in a reasonable timeframe.

How This Bad Habit Hurts Your Productivity

Applying overly-lenient time limits to tasks - or refusing to set time limits at all - makes you less productive in six ways. First, you end up getting fewer things done. Because each task takes you more time to complete, you have less time to work on other items.

Second, there's an increased risk of neglecting important tasks. As you plod through your to-do list, taking more time than necessary to finish items, high-priority tasks may never receive the attention they need.

Third, you'll run the risk of having to carry forward unfinished items. As we noted in Day 3, that leads to increased stress, which, in turn, makes it more difficult to work productively.

Fourth, your workflow will lack structure. Lenient time limits are usually arbitrary. We set them according to our comfort level. For example, we might give ourselves 2 hours to complete an assignment we know can be completed in 1 hour with focus and discipline. The lack of structure makes it easier for us to waste time.

Fifth, there's no sense of urgency. Without that urgency, we're more likely to take a casual approach to our workday. In other words, we dawdle.

Sixth, because we're getting less done, we end up working longer hours. Over an extended period, that not only increases our stress levels, but sets the stage for burnout.

Change comes from developing and reinforcing new habits. That's good news because it means you're in control. With that in mind, here are seven things you can do today to start completing tasks in less time.

Action Steps

1. Select a task from your to-do list and set a challenging time limit for it. If you're not sure how long the task should take you to complete, start with an estimate. You can change it later. The important thing is to get into the habit of working under self-imposed time limits.

2. Use a kitchen timer. Set it to count down the minutes, and position it so you can see it while you work. It will provide a constant reminder that time is slipping away. You may prefer to use your phone or computer to count down the time. Either option is fine. Personally, I prefer a loud kitchen timer. There's something about its "old-school" look that motivates me to work.

3. Use the Pomodoro Technique. The basic method is to work for 25 minutes and then take a 5-minute break. The idea is to break your workday into small chunks of time. The 5-minute breaks give your brain a chance to rest, which increases your focus and efficiency during the 25-minute work periods.

   Another advantage of using the Pomodoro Technique is that it gives you a way to monitor your progress on the task at hand. For example, if you've allocated 40 minutes to complete a task and you're less than halfway done after a single Pomodoro, you'll know you need to speed up.

4. Ignore email, social media, texts and phone calls. Ignoring distractions is always important when you're trying to work productively, but doubly so when you're working under challenging time limits. You don't have the luxury of surrendering to them. If you're using the Pomodoro Technique, wait until your 5-minute breaks to address them.

5. Commit to ending your workday at 5:00 p.m. Doing so will give you the impetus to meet your task-specific time limits.

   I mentioned earlier that getting less done during the day often translates into longer work hours. Don't give yourself that option. Decide in advance to walk away at 5:00 p.m.

6. Track your progress. As noted above, when you first start applying time limits to tasks, you'll have to estimate how long they should take to complete. By tracking your progress, you'll gain better insight.

   For example, suppose your boss needs you to complete a weekly report. You may have to guess the amount of time you'll need to finish it during the first week. By the fifth week, however, you'll be able to set a reasonable time limit based on your experience during the previous four weeks.

7. Adjust your time limits. As you work on the same tasks over and over, you'll be able to complete them in less time. That's due to improved competency. Don't be content to continue working according the time limits you set in the past. Revise them so they pose a challenge. Impose a sense of urgency to further increase the speed at which you work.

Day 5

Stop Kicking Yourself
Over Past Mistakes And Failures

Harvey Mackay, bestselling author of *Swimming With The Sharks Without Being Eaten Alive*, had the following to say about beating yourself up over past mistakes.

“ Worrying about the past or the future isn't productive. When you start chastising yourself for past mistakes, or seeing disaster around every corner, stop and take a breath and ask yourself what you can do right now to succeed.”

That's smart advice. Berating yourself leads to discouragement. It also makes you wary of taking risks. You become risk-averse, gripped by an ever-growing fear of failure.

In most jobs, relationships and personal pursuits, fear of failure is a liability. It impairs our ability to make decisions. It holds us back from accomplishing the goals we set for ourselves.

That's the effect of dwelling on mistakes you've made in the past. You end up recoiling from challenges, and thereby stunting your personal and professional growth.

Your productivity also suffers a major blow.

How This Bad Habit Hurts Your Productivity

Regret is normal since mistakes are a part of life. It can even be beneficial if it's experienced in the context of introspection. Self-analysis helps us to learn more about ourselves and make positive changes that lead to better outcomes.

Having said that, brooding over your mistakes, overthinking them to the point of despair, is unhealthy. It can hobble your ability to work productively in four ways.

First, it's easy to become consumed by your past failures. You become wracked by guilt, which dominates your thoughts.

Second, the more you obsess about your mistakes, the less likely you'll forgive yourself. That unforgiving attitude can erode your motivation to work. You'll needlessly spend time rebuking yourself rather than working on the tasks and projects on your to-do list.

Third, mental self-flagellation will eventually affect your health. Studies have shown that negative thoughts and emotions can have an adverse effect on our physical well-being. Over time, such thoughts and emotions set the stage for depression and feelings of helplessness. It's difficult to be productive when you feel like you have no control over your life.

The fourth way kicking yourself for past failures impedes your productivity is that it causes you to miss out on opportunities. You spend so much time being angry with yourself and remaining fearful of making mistakes that you fail to act on things that might help you to get things done. For example, you might avoid asking your boss for direction on a project if you feel unworthy of his or her attention given your past mistakes.

Change starts today. Below, you'll find seven Action Steps that will help you to forgive yourself, let go of past failures and move on with your life.

Action Steps

1. Embrace failures as learning opportunities. Doing so requires having (or developing) a growth mindset. That's an attitude that approaches setbacks as chances to improve specific areas of your life. It takes time to develop this perspective. Rest assured, your life will change once you do.

2. Look for opportunities to improve your workflow. Failure is feedback about something you're doing. That something is either working or not working. Whenever you fail, ask yourself whether there's a better approach.

   For example, suppose past projects have stalled due to your lack of knowledge or expertise. Ask yourself if you should research things before starting work on future projects.

3. Acknowledge your role in making the mistake. At first, this might seem to contradict the advice give above. After all, acknowledging your role is akin to beating yourself up over it, right? Not necessarily. Instead, you're recognizing that you're in control. Being in control means you can influence outcomes. In this case, that means being proactive and taking steps to improve your approach to work.

4. Reevaluate your expectations. The tendency to kick yourself over past mistakes may stem from holding yourself to overly-high standards. Are you trying to be perfect? Or do you give yourself enough latitude to make mistakes now and again?

5. Reevaluate your goals. Make certain they're realistic and complement your workflow.

   For example, suppose you've imposed an aggressive deadline on yourself for a report needed by your boss. First, ask yourself if the deadline is realistic given your other responsibilities. Then, ask yourself whether your method of working will accommodate your deadline. If not, make adjustments - either to your deadline or your workflow.

6. Avoid television. Binge-watching your favorite shows may seem appealing if you're down on yourself. But it can worsen your situation.

   Earlier, I mentioned that dwelling on past mistakes sets the stage for depression. Now consider that studies show binge-watching TV can lead to the same state. Your favorite television programs won't help you to feel better. They'll just help you to ignore the root cause of your despair.

7. Talk to a peer, mentor or accountability partner. If you're feeling angry toward yourself, discuss your feelings with someone whose advice you trust.

   Don't use the opportunity to vent. Instead, take advantage of the other person's objectivity. Because that individual isn't emotionally involved, he or she will have a more grounded perspective concerning your self-punishment.

Day 6

Stop Saying "Yes" To Everyone

In his book *The Distinguishing Mark of Leadership*, author Don Meyer quotes Warren Buffet as saying the following:

❝ The difference between successful people and very successful people is that very successful people say 'no' to almost everything."

Buffet's remark mirrors a comment made by Steve Jobs while giving a presentation at the Apple Worldwide Developers Conference (WWDC) in 1997. He noted:

❝ Focusing is about saying no."

Most people say yes. They acquiesce when a stranger asks for their time. They give in when a coworker asks for help. They surrender when a family member demands immediate attention.

On the surface, such a response seems reasonable. After all, a willingness to help others is an admirable quality. The problem is, saying "yes" forces us to put our own tasks and responsibilities on the back burner. Every moment we devote to helping someone is a moment we cannot allocate toward getting our own work done.

Constantly saying "yes" has another adverse effect: you gain a reputation for being helpful. Again, that seems admirable. But consider: making yourself available to anyone who asks only encourages people to seek your help in the future. It's like placing a bowl of milk on your doorstep for stray cats. As long as you continue to provide the milk, the stray cats will come. Guaranteed.

Let's take a closer look at how the habit of saying "yes" diminishes your ability to get things done.

How This Bad Habit Hurts Your Productivity

Yielding to others' demands for your time and attention lessens your productivity in five ways. First, it disrupts your work flow. You lose whatever momentum you managed to build through focused attention. Without distractions, that momentum helps you to complete tasks in less time.

Second, it allows other people to dictate how you spend your time. You're never in charge of your day, which means you can't accurately plan it. Indeed, any plans you make are little more than wishes, or best-case scenarios.

Third, saying "yes" gives you less time to address your own responsibilities. That can be disastrous if you're working under an impending deadline. The people you help benefit by completing their tasks, but your own tasks remain unfinished. You may even be forced to work overtime to meet your responsibilities (see Day 7 for more on this bad habit).

Fourth, it reduces the quality of your work. After spending considerable time helping others meet *their* responsibilities, you may be forced to rush through your own in order to finish them under deadline. The more you rush, the greater the likelihood you'll make mistakes. While one or two mistakes are unlikely to cause a major problem, work littered with them will.

Fifth, you risk suffering from burnout. Continuously relenting to others' demands increases your stress levels. Deadlines loom and your work piles up as you spend your available time helping coworkers with their tasks. It's tough to be productive when you're feeling overstretched and under pressure.

Let's make a change. Following are seven steps to take if you want to learn to say "no" to your coworkers, friends and family members.

Action Steps

1. Evaluate your progress regarding the tasks on your to-do list before offering to help other people. Note how much time you've allocated to each task and determine whether you have enough time left in the day to address them as planned. If you're ahead of schedule, offer your help to the person asking for it. Otherwise, tactfully say "no" and explain your reason.

   Obviously, there's nothing wrong with helping people. You should do so whenever you can. But you need to make sure you're not jeopardizing the quality or timeliness of your own work in the process.

2. Remind yourself that few requests are truly emergencies. People seeking help usually want to receive it immediately. Their urgency rarely stems from a crisis. Rather, most people simply want whatever they seek sooner rather than later. It's human nature.

   Before offering your help, determine whether a true crisis exists that warrants your swift attention. Again, most "emergencies" aren't emergencies at all.

3. Ask whether you can help the person later. That allows you to say "no" and simultaneously appear willing to accommodate the

individual. This approach also helps you to retain control of your time, a crucial part of working productively.

People who hear this response will find it to be more palatable than a simple "no."

4. Find out what you're being asked to commit yourself to. When people ask for help, they often downplay the amount of time it will take. For example, consider the times you've heard someone ask you, "Got a second for a quick question?"

Ask the person seeking your help to clearly describe what he or she wants you to do for them. If the tasks involved require more time than you have to offer, you'll have a suitable reason to decline.

5. Decide in advance the activities you won't help others with. Placing limits on the types of work you're willing to address will make it easier to rebuff requests for help.

For example, you might decide to shun making phone calls before 10:00 a.m. because you know such calls expose you to potential time sinks. A planned 3-minute call can easily turn into 20 minutes if the person you've called is chatty. If a coworker asks you to call a vendor or client for him or her, tactfully decline and explain your reason.

6. Practice saying "no," even if you have the time to help the other person. This may seem unkind and selfish. But as with every bad habit profiled in this book, making a positive change requires developing a new habit to replace the harmful one.

Forming a new habit takes time and practice. It takes repeated application, a theme that runs through this entire action guide.

Be graceful, but steadfast. Saying "no" will become easier with time.

7. Work in time blocks. Set aside chunks of time during which you are not to be disturbed.

For example, if you're using the Pomodoro Technique, you could set aside a 2-hour block. That would cover four 25-minute Pomodoros and their attendant 5-minute breaks.

The key to making this work is to clearly communicate to others that you'll be unavailable during these 2-hour periods. If someone "forgets" and approaches to ask for your help, gently remind him or her that you're unavailable. Let that person know when your time block ends, and ask him or her to return at that time.

Day 7

Stop Working Overtime

A typical workweek in the U.S. spans 40 hours. That's due, in large part, to Henry Ford. Back when Ford was making a mint with his Model Ts, he experimented with the number of hours worked per day and the number of days worked per week by his employees. At the time, his employees were putting in 48 hours or more over a six-day week. For some, a normal workday lasted more than 10 hours.

On January 5, 1914, Ford made a progressive decision. He cut the number of hours worked per day to eight and reduced the number of days worked per week to five. At the same time, he doubled his workers' pay.

From that point on, any time spent at work in excess of 40 hours per week was deemed "overtime."

Ford's decision revealed an important insight about workers' productivity. He found that reducing both the number of hours worked per day and the number of days worked per week increased his workforce's output.

Today, millions of people work overtime on a regular basis. If you're one of them, you're not working at your peak level of productivity. Worse, the more overtime you put in week after week, the less productive you are.

It's not your fault. Your work-related obligations may require you to put in 60 or more hours per week. But realize that over the long run, doing so will cause you to become less effective at your job. The long hours will slowly eat away at your efficiency, energy levels and focus.

How This Bad Habit Hurts Your Productivity

Working overtime is a common problem in the U.S. Despite research showing that reducing work hours increases productivity, many companies encourage their employees to log an unreasonable number of hours each week. Similarly, many small business owners feel they need to put in long hours to compete in their respective industries.

The persistent overtime makes you less productive in four ways.

First, it sets the stage for health issues. Studies show that workers who put in a substantial number of hours each week are more prone to back aches, weight problems and hypertension. They're also more susceptible to cardiac events.

Second, it can raise your stress levels. Research has shown that elevated stress that persists for an extended period of time dramatically reduces our productivity.

In 2014, professional services firm Towers Watson conducted a study involving 22,347 employees in the U.S., UK and 10 other countries. The researchers found that employees experiencing high levels of stress were more likely to report workplace disengagement. A Towers Watson consultant noted that the findings demonstrated "the destructive link between high levels of stress and reduced productivity."

Third, working too many hours opens the door to burnout. You may experience headaches, digestive problems, chest pain and even signs of depression as your stress levels rise. Worse, burnout happens slowly, so you're unlikely to notice early signs that indicate a problem. The longer you put in extra hours, the more likely you'll suffer these symptoms, all of which will ultimately derail your productivity.

The fourth way overtime can harm your productivity is that it causes you to produce a lower quality of work. When you feel stressed, discouraged and worn out, you're more likely to cut corners. With time, you'll start to resent your work along with your inability to care enough about it to do a good job.

Below, you'll find five action steps that will help you to break the overtime habit and regain control of your workflow.

Action Steps

1. Make sure your to-do list is reasonable given the amount of time you have available.

   On Day 3, we talked about the tendency to create overly-ambitious to-do lists. While most people carry forward unfinished tasks (a problem in and of itself), some burn the midnight oil in an attempt to complete them. Avoid that scenario by limiting your to-do list to five high-priority items.

2. Plan to log five productive hours at most during any given eight-hour day. Most people assume they'll be able to put in a full eight hours of work. But that's highly optimistic. Between the disruptions and distractions you'll face in the workplace (or at home), a significant amount of time will slip away from you.

   Plan your day with the assumption that you'll turn in five hours of productive work. Make sure your to-do lists are realistic given that expectation.

3. Be willing to leave unfinished tasks on your desk. Some people are so strongly opposed to doing so that they're willing to sacrifice sleep in order to finish the assignments.

Don't make that mistake. If an uncompleted task can be left for tomorrow, leave it.

4. Schedule breaks. It sounds simple. But taking breaks is often a challenge for individuals who pride themselves on their work ethic. The problem is, working through your breaks comes with a major downside: your mind never gets an opportunity to rest. Without rest, it can't work efficiently.

Take breaks. Then, come back to your work feeling refreshed so you can focus on it.

5. Commit to finishing the workday at a specific time. For example, pledge to call it quits at 5:00 p.m. Don't agree to meetings that extend beyond that time. And don't take work home with you.

That may seem impossible if you have a tough boss or a mountain of responsibilities. But aside from unreasonable circumstances, there's usually room for flexibility. Be proactive and make changes to your workflow.

For example, shorten your to-do list (Day 3). Rebuff others' demands for help (Day 6). Overcome your tendency to procrastinate (Day 10). Make whatever adjustments are necessary to help you to end each day at 5:00 p.m.

Day 8

Stop Being A Control Freak

When we're put in charge of projects, it can be tough to delegate items to other people. Doing so means letting go of control. That can be scary, particularly if we're the ones who'll be in the hot seat if the tasks we delegate are handled poorly.

That's the perspective of a control freak. It's not irrational. But it can have major consequences in terms of workplace productivity and staff efficiency.

The control freak does everything in his or her power to keep a tight rein on whatever project is on their plate. He or she isn't content to delegate and supervise. The control freak must micromanage, ensuring every detail is addressed properly and in a timely fashion.

It's an exhausting way to work. It's also likely to hinder the project manager's effectiveness and erode the morale of his or her team.

The tendency to avoid delegating tasks isn't just the province of corporate managers. Small business owners and freelancers face the same temptation. In fact, entrepreneurs are notorious for being control freaks. Many have grown accustomed to doing everything themselves to make their businesses successful. That inclination has been reinforced in their psyches to such an extent that they're all but unable to cede control to others.

That's a problem. If you're trying to do everything yourself, you cannot possibly work at peak productivity.

How This Bad Habit Hurts Your Productivity

The negative effects of being a control freak aren't always obvious, at least not to the person trying to retain control. In most cases, he or she fails to realize they're doing more harm than good - to themselves, their work output and their company or business.

It's important that we highlight some of the ways doing everything on your own inhibits your productivity. Four are worth noting here. First, being a control freak siphons away time and resources from your other responsibilities. Your attention is instead devoted to micromanaging every minute detail.

Second, you're less focused on your long-term goals. Being overly involved in the minutiae of your project means you're less attentive of the big picture.

For example, if you're a corporate manager, the big picture might be to complete your project in such a way that it allows integration with other departments in your company. If you're an entrepreneur, the big picture might involve growing your business to the point that you can obtain venture capital. You can't focus on these objectives if your time is monopolized by trivial details.

Third, the quality of your work will decline. You cannot do everything yourself and expect to maintain high quality standards over the long run. You don't have enough time or energy. Attempting to do so is a recipe for burnout.

The fourth effect of being a control freak impacts those who report to you: your employees, vendors and contractors. Micromanaging their tasks and responsibilities shows them you have little faith in their skills and competence. That breeds mistrust and resentment, both of which damage your team's morale.

There's considerable value in quelling your inner control freak and learning how to delegate tasks effectively. Following are several tips that will help you to accomplish both goals.

Action Steps

1. Identify your reasons for wanting to maintain control. Do you doubt others in their ability to perform certain tasks? Do you fear that delegating tasks will cause others to think of you as nonessential to your organization? Are you a perfectionist (see Day 2 for more information) and want to ensure zero errors? The only way to curb your inner control freak is to determine why you feel the need to be in control of everything.

2. Separate "big picture" tasks from "operational" tasks. Every project is comprised of two types of to-do items: those that have long-range effects and those that have short-range effects. They rank differently in importance.

   For example, your job as a manager might be to see your team's current project through to completion within the time and budgetary constraints established before the project began. That's a long-range, or "big picture," item. The day-to-day tasks, such as running reports and following up with vendors, should be delegated to your employees. Whether you're a corporate manager, freelancer, small business owner or serial entrepreneur, it's important to have that perspective to squelch the temptation to micromanage.

3. Determine how much an hour of your time is worth. Doing so will give you a barometer by which to gauge whether the time you're spending on a specific task would be better spent elsewhere.

   Your goal, whether you're a manager or entrepreneur, is to spend your time where it will yield the greatest return. Calculating your hourly rate gives you an easy-to-use yardstick.

4. Track how you use your time throughout the workday. You may find that you're spending an inordinate amount of time on tasks that should be delegated to others.

Track your time for two weeks. That will smooth out inconsistencies that occur from one day to the next, and reveal trends in your time usage. You can use an online tool like Toggl.com (it's free and integrates with your phone) or a pad of paper. The medium is unimportant. What matters is that you track your time and analyze how you use it.

5. Keep notes on people to whom you can delegate tasks. Effective delegation entails identifying employees or contractors you can trust to do a job well. If you've worked with certain people before, you should have a good idea regarding their skill sets and areas of competence. Your job is to delegate items to them according to their experience, expertise and talent.

Don't trust your memory. Keep notes you can refer to later when you need to outsource a task. Evernote.com is a good tool for this purpose.

6. Explain the big picture to the person to whom you're delegating a task. The tendency to micromanage usually stems from a lack of confidence in others. One way to develop that confidence is to convey to others how their efforts will contribute to the end goal.

For example, rather than simply telling an employee to create a specific report, explain to the individual how the report will help the company save money. Rather than telling a web designer to build a website for your business, explain what you want the website to do in terms of branding and functionality.

7. Delegate one task today. Letting go of control is uncomfortable. It takes practice. The only way to develop this new habit is through repeated application.

Start slowly by trusting a member of your team to handle a simple task you would otherwise handle yourself. It's okay to monitor his or her progress. But give the individual enough autonomy to do the work for you.

Day 9

Stop Eating Unhealthy Foods

In 2012, a study conducted by the Health Enhancement Research Organization, Brigham Young University and the Center for Health Research at Healthways revealed an interesting relationship between diet and productivity. The authors found that workers following an unhealthy diet were 66% more likely to experience a significant decline in productivity compared to their healthy-eating peers.

That finding shouldn't come as a surprise. You know intuitively that your diet affects your work. Chances are, you've seen the effects firsthand. You're more productive when eating healthy meals than you are when following a diet composed of pizza, donuts, chips and ice cream.

To understand the reasons, it's necessary to appreciate how our brains respond to food. Our bodies are proficient at breaking down the foods we eat into glucose. Our brains need glucose in order to function. That's the reason you feel drowsy and have difficulty concentrating when you're hungry. The amount of glucose available to your brain has been depleted.

Scientists have found that the optimal level of glucose in the bloodstream is 25 grams. That's the amount that should be circulating through our bodies at all times. When the amount drops below 25 grams, the brain functions at a suboptimal level.

Most people realize that glucose is simply sugar. So they grab a sugary snack or carb-filled meal when they start to feel drowsy. The problem is, such foods cause glucose levels to quickly spike and plummet. Rather than fueling your brain with the glucose it needs to function throughout the day, such foods provide less than 30 minutes of mental acuity. After that 30 minutes, you "crash." Your blood sugar levels decline and you become drowsy and unfocused again.

Clearly, that's a less-than-ideal predicament if you're trying to boost your productivity.

How This Bad Habit Hurts Your Productivity

A poor diet does much more than just make you feel lethargic. It can severely impede your ability to get things done.

First, junk food makes it harder for you to focus. If you're unable to think clearly, you'll be less likely to stay on task. You'll also be more inclined to succumb to distractions.

Second, poor dieting habits make you less alert. As mentioned above, you become drowsy as your blood glucose levels fall. That's a common outcome after eating a sugar-laden meal or snack. Over the long run, persistently-low glucose levels can lead to chronic fatigue, severely hampering your productivity.

Third, an unhealthy diet will adversely affect your decision-making skills. Your ability to make sound decisions is heavily influenced by whether your brain is receiving the glucose and nutrients it needs to function properly. A bad diet won't provide the materials your brain needs.

A fourth side effect is lower energy levels. Junk food can make you feel more energized - for 30 minutes. That's because such foods are quickly converted into glucose. But the level of glucose drops just as quickly, siphoning your energy with it. You've no doubt seen this effect in children who are given candy. They're filled with energy (thanks to the sugar) for a brief period that precipitates a crash.

Fifth, poor nutrition sets the stage for increased anxiety; certain foods can trigger and aggravate stress. Numerous studies have shown that high stress levels negatively affect a person's focus and effectiveness. Meanwhile, the more stress you experience, the more likely you are to eat unhealthy food.

It's a destructive cycle. Worse, its effect on your productivity happens gradually, so it's difficult to detect.

To change your dieting habits, replacing unhealthy foods for healthy alternatives, follow the five action steps listed below.

Action Steps

1. Make a list of healthy foods and use it as the foundation of your diet.

    We have more culinary options available to us today than ever in history. That comes with a major downside: unhealthy foods are always within reach. If you're a sugar addict, the temptation to grab a sugary snack when you feel the first pangs of hunger is nearly irresistible.

    To counter the temptation, create a short list of healthy meals to eat. Limit your list to five options. Restricting your choices will make you less inclined to entertain eating unhealthy foods. If a certain type of food doesn't make it onto your list, avoid it.

2. Make a list of healthy snacks. Whenever you feel hungry outside your normal mealtimes, pick something off your list. The goal is to make it easy to select something nutritious.

    As with your list of healthy meals (Action Step #1), limit your healthy-snack list to five options.

3. Make a list of foods and snacks to avoid. All of us have food vices. For me, it's ice cream. You may prefer cookies, cupcakes or potato chips. Create a list of your personal vices and put it somewhere within reach.

When I began to change my diet, I carried an index card in my wallet. My food weaknesses were listed on the card as a constant reminder. That approach may work for you too.

4. Plan the week's meals. If you're not sure what to eat, you'll be more likely to eat whatever is convenient and available. That's one of the main draws of fast food. To resist the temptation, plan your meals ahead of time. Know what you'll be eating for breakfast, lunch and dinner for the entire week. If possible, fix your meals in advance.

For example, I cook seven to eight pounds of chuck roast at a time. Most of it goes into the freezer. Some goes into the refrigerator where it's always available for a quick, easy-to-fix meal.

5. Create an eating schedule. Routines bring order to our day. Eating at the same times each day lessens the likelihood that you'll grab whatever is within reach when you're hungry. That includes the candy bar from the vending machine and the donuts your coworker brought to the office.

Day 10

Stop Procrastinating

The procrastination habit harms your productivity more than any other bad habit. Unfortunately, it's one of the most difficult to break.

We learn to put things off as children, setting aside our school assignments and chores in order to play with our friends. For most of us, that habit continued into adulthood. We've become adept at postponing tasks that warrant our attention in favor or more immediately-gratifying activities.

We procrastinate for many reasons. Some of us do it because we fear failure. We defer taking action because we don't want to botch the job and look foolish to our bosses or peers. Others stall because they're perfectionists (see Day 2). They fear turning in work that is imperfect, and so put tasks off indefinitely. Still others procrastinate due to the pressure they feel to perform. The pressure stimulates an aversion to whatever task is in front of them.

There are, of course, other reasons we drag their feet on projects. Many of us have poor time management skills. We fail to plan our days properly and thus allow time to slip through our fingers. Left with little time to spend on the projects we're responsible for, we put them off until later.

Some of us are caught in the crossfire of an ongoing battle between our limbic system and prefrontal cortex. The limbic system is the part of our brain that's drawn to shiny baubles. It will drop critical tasks without warning to attend to the most trivial distractions. The prefrontal cortex is the accountant of the brain. It's where executive functions, such as planning, are carried out. These two areas fight for control of your attention. The outcome is influenced by your level of focus. If you're completely focused on a task, your prefrontal cortex will gain the upper hand. If you're bored or disengaged, your limbic system will win, and you can expect your productivity to take a hit.

How This Bad Habit Hurts Your Productivity

Putting things off occasionally is fine. In fact, doing so is healthy if you've been working with your nose to the grindstone for an extended period. Setting the task at hand aside gives your brain a chance to rest and recuperate. The problem is, habitual procrastinators put things off as a norm. They do it as a matter of course from day to day.

That habit has a profound effect on your productivity. First, it increases your stress level. When you initially set tasks aside, you experience *less* stress. That's understandable since the delayed task is set aside for a more gratifying activity. But over the long run, your stress level rises due to the consequences of deferring action (you have more work to do with less time to do it).

Second, you forfeit valuable time. You're not going to allocate the time you earned by postponing work on task A to work on task B. If you're like most people, you'll spend the time doing things you enjoy, such as watching cat videos on YouTube.

Third, you'll miss deadlines. The tasks and projects you postponed won't magically disappear. You'll still need to address them at some point. The problem is, you'll have less time to do so. Consequently, you may end up turning work in late, tarnishing your reputation - or grades if you're in school - in the process.

Fourth, habitual procrastination increases the likelihood that you'll miss important opportunities. For example, postponing action on an assigned report for your boss requires that you spend time later to complete it. As a result, you may be unavailable later to contribute to a high-profile project that would give you exposure to senior partners at your company.

Ongoing procrastination can also lead to self-loathing. The more tasks you put aside, and the more consequences you face (for example, missed deadlines and missed opportunities), the more you'll wonder why you're always found wanting. That kind of self-reproach can grind down your self-esteem.

Below, you'll find six action steps designed to help you clobber the procrastination habit.

Action Steps

1. Modify your to-do list. First, make sure it's not overly-ambitious (see Day 3 for more information). Trim items wherever possible. Second, assign a high priority to the most important tasks of the day.

2. Develop a clearly-defined work schedule. Organize your day into time blocks with each block devoted to working on a certain task or group of related tasks. Choose blocks of time that accommodate your energy levels and work style.

    For example, I use the Pomodoro Technique. That entails working for 25 minutes, and then taking a 5-minute break (I follow a modified version to complement my workflow). You may prefer to work for three hours at a time followed by a 30-minute break. The important thing is to define the boundaries for yourself.

3. Find ways to stay busy. Ben Franklin once said "if you want something done, ask a busy person." There's wisdom in that quote. Busy people know how to manage their time. They don't have a choice. As a result, they're habitual action takers.

The idea behind keeping busy is that you'll force yourself to take action as more to-do items pile up on your plate.

4. Break down large projects into bite-sized tasks. A common reason people procrastinate is because they feel overwhelmed. They're confronted with a huge project and are paralyzed by it. It's like standing at the base of Mount Everest and not knowing how to climb it. The solution is to break the job down into small, individual tasks.

For example, suppose you're responsible for producing a 100-page report for your boss. That's a major project. Rather than becoming discouraged by its scope, break it down into small, manageable parts. List the types of spreadsheets and graphs you'll need to create. List the types of data you'll need for the spreadsheets and graphs, along with their respective sources. Once you've broken the job down, schedule due dates for the individual tasks. The project will seem less daunting and you'll feel more in control.

5. Identify a *reason* for each task or project. Knowing why something needs to be done often provides the motivation needed to take action. Even habitual procrastinators can be prompted to take action when they assign meaning to projects they dread.

6. Seek accountability. Many people are more inclined to act when they know others are expecting them to do so. If you're similarly motivated, you'll benefit from having an accountability partner.

This person is there to hold your feet to the fire. If you fail to do what you pledged to do, your accountability partner will ask the reason. The prospect of having to admit failure may be enough to spur you to action.

Day 11

Stop Postponing Taking Action On Hard Tasks

We tend to postpone tasks we expect to be difficult or unpleasant. That's human nature. Everyone does it. For example, we might happily take our dogs for a 30-minute walk, but cringe at the thought of spending 30 minutes doing yard work.

That tendency carries consequences. We get less done, focus on the wrong things and even develop a foreboding sense of failure for repeatedly putting off important items.

And of course, our to-do lists continue to grow as difficult and unpleasant tasks linger on them, carried forward day after day.

There are two schools of thought concerning how to solve this issue. Some folks advocate tackling the hardest tasks on your to-do list first, before you address simpler or more enjoyable items. Other folks advise the opposite - work on a few easy tasks to get your momentum and then focus on the harder items.

Both approaches have merit. Both can be effective. Everyone works differently; the strategy that works best for you may be a poor fit for someone else.

I'll give you several action steps in a moment that will help you to figure out which approach is best-suited to you. First, however, let's take a look at how the tendency to postpone difficult tasks hurts your productivity.

How This Bad Habit Hurts Your Productivity

As I mentioned yesterday, postponing tasks doesn't make them disappear. They remain on your to-do list where they constantly demand your attention. Worse, each one points an accusatory finger at you, chiding you for your lethargy.

Over time, tasks that should have been completed - or at least started - days or weeks prior begin to take an emotional toll. First, you'll experience increased anxiety as your once-manageable to-do list grows out of control.

Second, you'll become increasingly frustrated. Each time you glance at your to-do list, you'll be reminded that you actively chose to postpone difficult items.

Third, you'll start to feel pangs of guilt and shame. Putting off hard tasks implies - fairly or otherwise - an inability to take action. You'll blame yourself for your apathy.

Fourth, the more anxiety, frustration and guilt you experience, the less focus you'll enjoy. You'll find it increasingly difficult to concentrate. That, in turn, will make you more susceptible to distractions.

Fifth, this bad habit can even lead to health problems. In 2015, the Journal of Behavioral Medicine published a study showing a link between postponing tasks and the onset of hypertension and cardiovascular disease.

Occasionally putting off tasks is sometimes necessary. And it's rarely a problem. But there's no question that it will hamper your productivity if you do it on a regular basis. With that in mind, here are several steps you can take today to break the habit.

Action Steps

1. Set aside an hour in the morning to work on one Big Rock. As we discussed in Day 3, your Big Rocks are the most important items on your to-do list. They may be difficult or unpleasant. But they must be addressed or bad things will happen.

   For example, suppose you're the CEO of a publicly-traded company. One of your Big Rocks might be to prepare a presentation for an upcoming meeting with your board of directors. If you fail to prepare, the board may lose faith in your ability to lead the company.

   Work on one of your Big Rocks during the first hour of your day. Don't worry about completing it. Just work on it for one hour. Doing so with the knowledge you'll be able to stop in 60 minutes will make the task seem less daunting.

2. Choose two Big Rocks for the day. That's it. No more than two.

   Most people overestimate the time they have available, and *underestimate* the time they'll need, to finish large or complex tasks. By limiting the number of Big Rocks you'll work on during any given day to two, you'll avoid overburdening yourself and destroying your motivation.

3. Start.

   That may sound pedestrian. But it's the hardest step, especially for tasks you expect to be difficult or unpleasant. Once you start working, it's relatively easy to *continue* working. Moreover, every moment you spend working on the task builds your momentum.

   For example, suppose your Big Rock is to clean your house.

Rather than dwelling on the time and effort needed to complete the entire job, start by wiping down your kitchen countertops. Then, clear off your living room coffee table. Then, wash the dishes sitting in your sink.

Just *start*. You may be surprised at how easy it is to continue working.

4. Expect obstacles. The greater the scope and complexity of a given task, the greater the likelihood you'll face stumbling blocks. Anticipate them. You'll save yourself frustration when they surface.

5. Be aware of how your brain tries to avoid hard tasks. It can be sneaky.

   For example, do you have a tendency to check Facebook whenever you're on the cusp of starting an unpleasant task? Or do you launch your favorite game on your phone to play for "a moment or two" before getting to work?

   Those are tactics your brain uses to shun difficult tasks. Once you identify them, you can take measures to hobble them. For example, the moment you notice the impulse to visit Facebook, acknowledge your brain's Pavlovian response and actively suppress it.

6. Set a time limit. One of the reasons difficult or complex tasks are daunting is because they often take a considerable amount of time to complete. Consequently, we shy away from them.

   Short-circuit that inclination by limiting the amount of time you'll commit to the task at hand. A time limit provides a definite ending point. It represents light at the end of the proverbial tunnel.

For example, rather than rolling up your sleeves and toiling away until the task at hand is complete, commit to working on it for 30 minutes. After 30 minutes have passed, decide whether to continue working on it - taking advantage of your momentum - or move on to another item on your to-do list.

Day 12

Stop Checking Social Media Throughout The Day

If you're like most people, you waste a lot of time on social media. There's no shame in it. Those sites are designed to appeal to your brain's tendency to procrastinate. They promise to take only a moment of your time. But you know that promise is a mirage. You know so because you've spent hours at a time browsing Facebook, Twitter, Instagram and the rest.

Again, it's not entirely your fault. Social media sites are built like Doritos - they're formulated to be addictive.

Let's take a look at some recent data to drive this point home.

According to Pew Research, 70% of Facebook users check in daily. That's neither surprising nor alarming. But the researchers go on to state that 45% check in *several times a day*. Likewise, 32% of Instagram users visit that site several times a day. Twenty-two percent of Twitter users are in the same boat.

Think about those figures for a moment. Also, consider that many of us have profiles at more than one social media site. That means we're visiting *multiple* sites several times each day. You can see how that might affect your productivity.

People are addicted to social media.

In 2010, the University of Maryland conducted a study and found that 18% of Facebook users were unable to go more than a few hours without visiting the site. Twenty-eight percent checked Twitter on their phones before getting out of bed in the morning.

Those data are consistent with research findings reported by Mobile Advertising Watch. The findings indicated that adults went on social media an average of *17 times a day*. And that's just using their phones! CNN reported in 2015 that many young people check social media more than 100 times a day.

Social media addiction is clearly a problem. Even if you're not addicted to Facebook, Twitter and Instagram, you're probably visiting them far too often. Unfortunately, that habit is wreaking havoc on your productivity.

How This Bad Habit Hurts Your Productivity

Going on social media numerous times throughout the day slows your workflow in five distinct ways. First, it's a constant distraction. You visit Facebook or Twitter to check whether your friends have posted anything new. But after you leave, you can't help but feel like you're missing out on something. That's the first sign of addiction.

Second, social media interrupts your workflow. Every interruption carries a switching cost. It takes at least 20 minutes to regain your momentum. That's the reason checking social media every hour (or even more frequently) prevents you from completing tasks. Doing so puts you in constant recovery mode.

Third, the ongoing distraction makes it difficult for you to concentrate on your work. Instead, your focus is on whatever you might be missing out on. The less focused you are, the less efficiently you'll be able to complete the tasks in front of you.

Fourth, social media shortens your attention span. Its immediacy (*"I must check in right now!"*) ends up influencing, and even dictating, your decisions concerning tasks you should address.

According to a study by Microsoft, the average adult attention span is only eight seconds, less than that of a goldfish. That's a marked decrease from 2000, when the average adult attention span was twelve seconds.

The fifth way social media affects your productivity is that it encourages procrastination. Checking in with friends on Facebook is more appealing than working on a report for your boss. Combined with the false promise that doing so will only take a few moments, the temptation to set aside your work is irresistible.

If the above reasons aren't enough to motivate you to break your social media habit, consider this: you're being manipulated by the top sites. In 2014, the New York Times reported that Facebook had been caught adjusting its users' feeds. The site changed the percentages of positive and negative items - in some cases, completely removing one or the other - to track the effect on users' emotions.

Social media isn't always a productivity killer. Checking in once or twice a day can even be beneficial as it gives your brain something unrelated to your work to focus on.

It's the constant draw of social media - for some, a true addiction - that's the problem.

Below, you'll find several action steps for curbing the habit.

Action Steps

1. Turn off all social media notifications. That includes your phone alerts as well as notifications delivered via your web browser. Even if you don't respond to the various pings, chirps and bells, they'll disrupt your concentration. Turn them off so you can work without interruption.

2. Set rules for yourself. First, limit the number of times you'll allow yourself to go on Facebook and other social media sites each day.

I recommend setting limits for both weekdays and weekends. Remember, you're building new habits. You need to be consistent to allow them to develop. Checking social media 100 times on Saturday and Sunday will undo the progress you made Monday through Friday.

Second, limit the number of minutes you'll allow yourself to spend on social media sites each day. Buy a kitchen timer and record the minutes you spend during each session. Keep a running tally so you'll know when you reach your daily limit. Over time, reduce the number of minutes to reclaim time you can devote to higher-priority tasks.

3. Schedule breaks. The longer you work without taking a break, the more prone you'll be to distractions. That's the reason time management experts recommend taking frequent breaks.

I've found that it's not enough for me to *plan* to take breaks. I have to schedule them. Otherwise, I'm apt to work through them, even though doing so has a negative effect on my long-term productivity.

Avoid making that mistake. Don't just tell yourself that you'll take breaks. Schedule them into your workday.

4. Use a site-blocking app. It allows you to designate certain sites (for example, Facebook) as potential time-wasters. The app will then prevent you from visiting those sites while you work. The amount of time you'll be blocked from them is up to you.

There are numerous site-blocking apps that work well. If you use Chrome, check the Chrome Web Store for StayFocusd. If you use Firefox, look for Leechblock. Or you can use apps designed for specific operating systems. For example, if you're on a Mac, check out SelfControl. If you're on a Windows machine, look for FocalFilter.

All of the above are free.

I'll be honest. I'm not a fan of using software designed to block sites. Why? Because I feel it's a band-aid approach to dealing with distraction. In my opinion, developing and reinforcing the positive habit of avoiding distraction when you should be working is a more effective long-term solution.

Having said that, many people swear by their site-blocking apps, and insist they're helpful. Test drive a few and decide for yourself.

5. Have a specific reason to check in. Social media is alluring because we can drift aimlessly from post to post and site to site with no real purpose. The downside is that we're tempted to do it over and over. It's akin to channel-surfing while watching television. With 500 channels at your fingertips, you can do it for hours on end. It's the same with social media.

Before you visit Facebook or Twitter, know your purpose for doing so. For example, do you want to get up to speed on a particular thread you've been following? Or would you like to see the latest tweets from your favorite celebrity? Or are you eager to check out your friend's wedding pictures? Have a reason to log on. Once you've satisfied the "itch," log off and return to your work.

Day 13

Stop Neglecting To Take Breaks

Imagine this scenario: you arrive at your office with a mile-long to-do list. A quick glance at your phone reveals that you have several voicemails waiting for your attention. And you don't have to check your email to know you've received several new messages, each representing a minor emergency.

It's going to be a busy day.

You consider squeezing in a quick lunch between afternoon meetings. Or, as an alternative, you can eat something during one of your scheduled conference calls.

But breaks? No way. There's no time.

That's the situation a lot of people find themselves in. Day after day, they're so busy at their jobs that they ignore their breaks. And life outside the workplace is often just as hectic.

A study by executive placement firm Right Management found that fewer than 20% of employees in the U.S. take an hour lunch. According to a survey conducted by staffing firm OfficeTeam, 29% work without taking a lunch at all.

We think we're too busy to take breaks. But in reality, that's rarely the case. Our days are harried because of overly-ambitious to-do lists (see Day 3), our tendency to say "yes" to others (see Day 6), our inclination to procrastinate (see Day 10) and other bad habits.

Additionally, many of us find that continuing to work is more appealing than taking a break. We don't want to forfeit our hard-won momentum.

The problem is, working without breaks decreases your productivity, making it more difficult for you to get things done in a reasonable time frame.

How This Bad Habit Hurts Your Productivity

Working without taking occasional recesses makes you less efficient in six ways. First, you're more likely to experience boredom as the day progresses. As you probably know from experience, boredom erodes your ability to focus. Diminished focus translates to reduced productivity.

Second, you're less likely to reflect on the headway you're making through your to-do list, and how it affects your goals. You become so immersed in the minutiae of your day that you're unable to see the big picture.

You've no doubt heard the expression "he can't see the forest for the trees." It describes the effect I'm referring to.

Third, your brain doesn't get a chance to rest and relax. That erodes your cognitive resources. That, in turn, impairs your creativity and ability to concentrate on the task at hand.

Fourth, neglecting to take breaks hampers your ability to commit important information to memory. Scientists have learned that the brain consolidates data and stores them in memory while we rest. Connections are made and memories form as our neurons communicate with each other.

This process doesn't occur - at least, not as efficiently - while we work. The result? Poor data retention.

The fifth way ignoring breaks hurts your productivity involves a psychological effect called vigilance decrement. At its simplest, it states that the brain's ability to focus deteriorates with each passing moment of continued attention. The more time you spend on a task, the less you'll be able to focus on it. Your brain experiences the law of diminishing marginal returns.

Sixth, working sans breaks increases the likelihood you'll "run out of juice" - both mentally and physically. It's no coincidence that workaholics often crash, suffering fatigue, back aches, stomach pains and other ailments.

If you've been neglecting taking breaks, now's the time to make a change. Following are five actionable tips you can put into practice today.

Action Steps

1. Schedule your breaks. If you don't schedule them, you're unlikely to take them, especially when you're juggling numerous projects and tasks. Commit to taking a short break - 5 or 10 minutes should suffice - according to a predefined timetable. For example, you might decide to take a 10-minute break after each 50-minute work session.

   Experiment with various work/break schemes. One popular approach is the 52/17 method. Work for 52 minutes and take a 17-minute break. Research shows that ultra-productive individuals stick closely to this routine.

   Some folks enjoy working in 90-minute blocks. They work for 90 minutes and then take a 20-minute break. I find this schedule doesn't work well for me. I start to lose focus at the 1-hour mark. But I encourage you to try it.

   Another popular approach is the Pomodoro Technique. Here, you work for 25 minutes followed by a 5-minute break. I prefer this method to others. I've even written an action guide describing how you can use it to streamline your workflow (you can find more information at the end of this book).

Try different approaches and choose the one that helps you to maximize your concentration.

2. Create a list of things to do on your breaks. That way, you'll feel as if your breaks have purpose. You'll enjoy a specific benefit by taking them.

For example, use the time to make dinner reservations and doctor appointments. Return calls from friends and family members (tell them you only have a few minutes before you have to return to work). Take a quick walk, grab a cup of coffee and listen to your favorite music. Read that magazine article that caught your eye days ago. Do a few simple exercises to get your blood flowing. Brainstorm ideas for a date night with your spouse.

If you have things planned for your breaks, you'll be more inclined to take them.

3. Create a list of things to *refrain* from doing on your breaks. Include activities that are tempting, but can impede your productivity over the long run.

For example, if you've spent the last two hours working on your computer, don't spend your break checking social media. Give your brain something else to do, preferably offline.

If you intend to eat something during your break, don't eat sugary snacks that will wreak havoc with your blood sugar levels. Grab something healthy.

The goal is to have a simple list you can refer to whenever you take a break. It will serve as a quick reminder of the activities you know will cause more harm than good.

4. Shed your guilt.

Many people feel guilty about taking breaks. Saddled with a heavy workload and others' expectations, they're unable to justify taking time off to rest. In most cases, the guilt they feel is completely unreasonable.

If you normally feel like you're doing something wrong by taking short recesses, it's important to identify the reasons. Only by doing so can you address them objectively and adopt healthier habits.

For example, does being idle for a few moments cause you to feel restless? If so, practice doing nothing until doing so becomes more comfortable. Do you feel ashamed taking a break when others need you to do things for them? If so, evaluate whether others' expectations are impractical.

Remind yourself that taking a few moments to relax every hour will improve your focus and productivity.

5. Set an alarm. If you decide to use the Pomodoro Technique, set the alarm for 25 minutes. That way, you'll be able to focus on the task in front of you without having to check the clock to make sure you take a break. The alarm will tell you when to do so.

I use a standard kitchen timer. You can also use your phone. Or if you work online, use your browser. Visit Google and type "timer 25 minutes" without the quotation marks. The important thing is that you use an actual timer to count down the time.

Day 14

Stop Binge-Watching Television Shows

❝ We owe a lot to Thomas Edison - if it wasn't for him, we'd be watching television by candlelight." - Comedian Milton Berle

It's America's favorite pastime.

According to Statistic Brain Research Institute, the average person watches more than five hours of television per day. That's equivalent to working a part-time job (of course, the downside is that you don't receive a paycheck). Over the average person's lifetime, he or she will watch nine years of TV!

Our penchant to reach for the remote stems from a variety of reasons. We want to relax after a hard day at the office. We want to leave behind the stress of the workday and escape into an engaging story. We hope to connect with the characters we see on our favorite shows, and perhaps experience a cathartic release as we identify with their challenges.

These motivations seem reasonable. After all, as we discussed yesterday (see Day 13), taking breaks is critical to maintaining productivity.

The problem is, we're inclined to binge. Many of us are wired that way. For example, I admit to bingeing on The Wire, Battlestar Galactica and 24. I've spent hours staring at the TV, wondering how 24's Jack Bauer will manage to survive the day. If you have a Netflix account or an Amazon Prime membership, you may be able to relate.

You're not alone.

According to a 2013 Harris Interactive study, 61% of surveyed Netflix users admitted to binge-watching their favorite shows on a regular basis. Moreover, 73% of that group expressed positive feelings about doing so.

But the habit carries a steep invoice. Findings from a study conducted by researchers at Ohio State University showed that excessive television watching can lead to depression. It can also open the door to back pain and weight gain. Research published in the medical journal Diabetologia indicated a day-long TV-binge session could increase the risk of diabetes by up to 30%.

Yet another side effect is even more alarming: decreased life expectancy. According to research published in the British Journal of Sports Medicine in 2011, each hour spent watching TV shaves 22 minutes off our lives.

It's clear binge-watching your favorite shows will affect your ability to get things done. Let's take a look at how it does so.

How This Bad Habit Hurts Your Productivity

Watching television rivals social media as the biggest time-waster of our generation. That might seem to be an alarmist claim. But recall from above that the average person will spend nine years of his or her life watching TV. That is a significant amount of productive time lost to passive entertainment.

Binge-watching has a negative effect on your mood and motivation. I mentioned earlier that too much time spent in front of the television has been linked to the onset of depression.

Even if you don't feel depressed, you're likely to feel lethargic and unmotivated after hours spent watching your favorite shows. Worse, the more you binge, the worse you feel until the thought of climbing off your couch fills you with dread.

Here's another reason binge-watching TV impairs your productivity: it's highly addictive. The magazine Scientific American ran an article in 2002 titled "*Television Addiction Is No Mere Metaphor.*" The authors compared TV watching to drug dependence, noting that both activities have a tranquilizing effect on the "user." They also found after reviewing multiple surveys that 10% of U.S. consumers considered themselves TV addicts. There is far more television programming available today compared to 2002. We can thus assume the problem remains just as prevalent.

Let's suppose you know you spend too much time watching TV. Would you be compelled to curb the habit if you knew it was having an adverse effect on your brain? A study published in the Archives of Pediatrics & Adolescent Medicine in 2010 linked toddlers' exposure to television to poor brain development and decreased classroom engagement.

While the study focused on how television affects children, it's reasonable to assume adults suffer similar effects. To that end, we know binge-watching can adversely impact adults' cognitive health through depression, insomnia and loneliness.

So, let's break the habit…

Action Steps

1. Identify your reasons for binge-watching television. You might assume you're doing it to relax or unwind after a tough day. But there may be an underlying trigger that warrants attention.

   For example, do you sometimes feel glum or dejected, and use TV as a way to put those feelings on the back burner? Do you often feel burnt out and see television as a tool that allows you to "unplug" from the stress in your life?

These are triggers. Spend 30 minutes to identify those that are driving you to your television.

2. Track how many hours per day you watch TV. It's possible you're underestimating the figure.

Over a two-week period, record the number of hours you spend watching your favorite shows each day. At the end of two weeks, you'll have a solid grasp of the amount of time that's slipping through your fingers.

3. Create a list of fun, rewarding activities you're unable to enjoy while watching TV. For example, every hour spent in front of your television is an hour you can't spend playing with your children or going on a date with your spouse. Likewise, you can't go hiking, have lunch with friends or work on growing your side business. You can't go to the gym, learn new skills or meet new people.

Keep this list nearby whenever you sit down to watch TV. It will motivate you to limit the time you spend sitting on your couch, or it might prompt you to skip television altogether.

4. Select three shows.

It's easy to binge-watch TV because there is so much high-quality programming available. I have friends who regularly watch 10 or more shows each week. That requires a massive investment of time.

Review a list of television shows you currently watch. Choose three and abandon the rest. It won't be easy. But it will pay dividends over the long run. You'll be floored by how much extra time you have at your disposal.

5. Limit the number of hours you allow yourself to watch TV each night. If you feel you currently watch too much, choose a number that is less than your current habit.

    For example, if you normally watch five hours of television per night, commit to watching *four* hours. After doing so become a habit, move the needle to *three* hours a night.

    The key is to start with a reasonable goal (e.g. four hours) and make progress by cutting back in small increments. Don't quit cold turkey, or cut your daily habit from five hours to one hour. Instead, set reasonable goals that deliver the same end result over a longer period of time.

6. Get rid of your televisions. Admittedly, I've never done this. But I once knew a man who did. He felt he was wasting his life watching television and took the most aggressive approach possible to curtail his habit.

    I mention this as an option, not a recommendation. Some folks do well by quitting cold turkey and discarding their TVs. I'm not one of them. If you're like me, I recommend following Action Step #6.

7. Reward your productivity with an hour of television. This tactic helps to ensure you get your work done before relaxing in front of your TV.

    Here, you're using television as an incentive. It's a treat. If you complete your to-do list, you get to watch your favorite show. Otherwise, you don't.

8. Cut your cable. Cable TV is where you'll find the most creative and engaging shows. From AMC's Breaking Bad and Showtime's Shameless to HBO's The Sopranos and FX's The Americans,

network television (ABC, NBC, etc.) can't compete - at least when it comes to storytelling. The downside is that the quality programming makes it difficult to break a deep-rooted TV addiction.

I recommend opting out of cable TV. Cut the cord. You'll not only recoup a significant amount of time, but you'll also save money on your cable bill.

Day 15

Stop Neglecting To
Create Systems For Recurring Tasks

Most people have to deal with tasks that repeat on a monthly, weekly or daily basis. Some deal with those that repeat several times throughout the day.

For example, you might be responsible for generating the same set of reports for your boss each morning. Or you might have to respond to the same set of questions from prospective customers. If you schedule a lot of corporate meetings, you may find yourself regularly fielding questions about their duration and content, along with the names of the participants.

Even if these fielding such questions are easy to do, they take time. And that's time you can't spend getting other things done.

For that reason, it's important to have systems in place. They can help to streamline the completion of these recurring tasks.

For example, suppose you maintain a blog. Chances are, you use Wordpress or a similar content management system (CMS). Such software was developed to systematize many of the activities involved with posting a blog or article online.

The systems you create may be much simpler depending on the repetitive tasks you want to streamline. For example, suppose one of your job responsibilities is to email job applicants about their resumes. Many of your emails will probably contain similar content. Why not create a template or form letter you can use for this purpose over and over?

Most people who face a large number of recurring tasks during the course of their day aren't doing enough to systematize them. Consequently, their productivity suffers a major blow.

How This Bad Habit Hurts Your Productivity

Without systems to streamline them, tasks that recur waste your time and mental energy. They demand your attention every time they need to be addressed. That affects your productivity in at least four ways.

First, repetition leads to boredom. Over time, that can siphon your motivation and eventually set the stage for burnout.

Second, when you address recurring tasks on an individual basis, you increase the degree of variability in your workflow. That variability erodes your efficiency, which, in turn, makes you less productive.

Third, you're more likely to make mistakes. Every task carries with it the possibility of committing an error. That's an acceptable risk when you're working on complex projects. Errors are expected. But they're difficult to justify for recurring tasks. After all, the fact that they repeat implies you possess a high level of proficiency in completing them. In reality, your boredom makes you less alert and more prone to making mistakes.

Fourth, not having systems in place to handle repetitive tasks forces you to spend too much time on them. Consider our earlier example of emailing job candidates about their resumes. Depending on the size of your company and the number of open positions, you could potentially waste hours each day addressing this single responsibility.

The action steps in the following section will help you to systematize the repetitive tasks that are currently hampering your productivity. It's likely you're already using a number of systems to streamline parts of your workflow. If that's the case, the following tips will help you to make them even more efficient.

Action Steps

1. Create a list of tasks that recur on a daily, weekly and monthly basis. This list will give you a bird's-eye view of such items and help you to brainstorm ways to streamline them.

2. Track how much time you spend performing monotonous tasks. This will motivate you to create systems for them.

   Setting up systems requires an investment of time. Many people postpone doing so because they don't realize how much time they waste addressing repetitive tasks. Tracking your time solves that problem. It will reveal how much of your day you actually spend on these items.

3. Batch recurring tasks that cannot be systematized. By doing so, you'll reduce the mental energy you spend completing them.

   Many repetitive tasks are small and take a minimal amount of time. But when addressed throughout the day, they serve as interruptions to your workflow. For example, you might spend 10 minutes each Wednesday afternoon emailing your company's newsletter to people on your mailing list. Or perhaps you spend a few minutes each Friday calling a particular vendor to order supplies. These tasks take little time, but can disrupt your momentum. Worse, there may be no way to automate them.

   Batch them together and work on them during a single block of time. Rather than spending 5 minutes here and 10 minutes there, set aside 45 minutes and complete all of the tasks during the same work session. You'll reduce distractions, improve your concentration and increase your efficiency.

4. Look for software that can help you to address recurring tasks.

I mentioned above that Wordpress, as a content management system, streamlines the chore of posting new blogs and articles to your website. That's an example of using software to systematize a recurring task. You still have to create the content (i.e. the blog or article), but Wordpress allows you to skip many of the technical steps involved with posting and formatting it.

Likewise, there's probably a way to automate, or at least streamline, some of your recurring tasks with software. For example, if you spend time each day transferring data from one spreadsheet into another, can you use formulas to do that job for you? If you're currently emailing customers to offer help after they purchase a product from your company, can you set up an online shopping cart to send out such emails automatically?

One of the core advantages of using software is that it streamlines our workflow. For example, I'm currently writing this chapter in a program called Scrivener. It organizes my content and makes exporting the material into various file formats a snap. No longer do I waste time wrestling with Microsoft Word.

Likewise, seek software that can help automate or streamline repetitive tasks that are currently disrupting your day.

5. Use Todoist to schedule recurring tasks. Reminding yourself to address these items is a chore unto itself. If you find yourself writing down the same task on each day's to-do list, realize there's a better way.

I mentioned Todoist in Day 3. I strongly recommend using this tool. It allows you to schedule repeating tasks so you'll be automatically reminded to handle them whenever they're due.

For example, suppose you need to complete a newsletter for your customers by the end of each Wednesday. In Todoist, create a new task and enter "every Wednesday" into the "due date" field. Todoist will add that item on each Wednesday's to-do list. You no longer have to manually add it.

By the way, this is an example of using software to streamline recurring tasks - in this case, adding repeating items to each day's to-do list.

6. Perform a monthly audit of your recurring tasks. Review each item and ask yourself whether it is essential to your goals.

Tasks that recur often occupy a workflow blind spot. We do them over and over, and thus grow accustomed to doing them. They become part of our routine. They become a habit. We seldom question whether they *need* to be done. We simply do them.

There may be items on your to-do list that can be eliminated without consequence. If so, purge them and save yourself time and energy.

Day 16

Stop Multitasking

" It turns out multitaskers are terrible at every aspect of multitasking." - Clifford Nass, Stanford University professor

We all do it. And according to scientists, we're all bad at it, even if we think otherwise.

The appeal of multitasking is twofold. First, we think we're getting a lot done, juggling multiple tasks and activities. Second, our sense of accomplishment gives us a good feeling.

But that perception is a mirage. In reality, we're not getting more things done in less time. If anything, multitasking *reduces* our productivity.

So why are we so drawn to its false promise? Researchers claim the reason involves our emotions.

In 2012, the Journal of Communication published findings from a study exploring the personal gratification people experience while performing multiple tasks at the same time. The authors found that despite the fact that "multitasking impairs task performance," people continue to do it because it makes them feel good.

That's why we're so drawn to it despite numerous studies demonstrating its negative impact on our productivity.

There are other reasons we multitask. Boredom is a common one. By addressing more than one task at the same time, we distract ourselves and thus feel less bored.

Impatience is also a trigger. Thanks largely to technology, life moves faster today than ever. Many of us can't sit still and focus on a single activity - for example, holding a conversation - because we feel we can be doing much more.

You might multitask to impress your boss. It's not your fault. Many employers encourage the practice. Some go so far as to tell job candidates that the ability to multitask is an expectation.

Lastly, many of us do it because we feel we're otherwise wasting time. After all, if we can cook dinner and talk on the phone while checking updates on Facebook and Twitter, why not do it?

The reason is because doing so hurts our productivity.

How This Bad Habit Hurts Your Productivity

In order to appreciate why multitasking impairs your productivity, it's important to understand how the brain processes decisions and actions.

Our brains line up activities and addresses them one by one. It may seem as if we're doing many things at once, but in reality, our brains are switching back and forth between tasks. That's important to understand because of the associated switching cost. That cost is defined in terms of how long the brain needs to shift its control settings to handle the next queued task. The more complex the tasks and the more they differ, the greater the cost.

The harm multitasking does to your productivity stems from this switching cost.

First, it obliterates your ability to concentrate. In addressing multiple things at once - or at least *seeming* to do so - you force your brain to repeatedly jump from one task to another. Consequently, you never have enough time to focus on any single task.

Second, evidence suggests multitasking has an adverse effect on your brain. Researchers at Stanford University found that the practice erodes cognitive control. Their findings were published in the journal *Proceedings of the National Academy of Sciences* in 2009.

Third, you're more vulnerable to distractions while multitasking. That shouldn't be a surprise. Increased susceptibility to distractions goes hand in hand with reduced concentration.

Fourth, switching costs (mentioned above) impede our progress, requiring us to take more time to complete tasks. They also increase the likelihood of errors, which, in turn, require time to correct.

Fifth, when we multitask, we're more inclined to cut corners in our work. Part of the reason stems from the additional time we need to complete tasks. With less time at our disposal, we begin to rationalize carelessness and shoddy output.

If you're a habitual multitasker, breaking the habit can be tough, even if you realize it's severely hampering your productivity. Following are six steps you can take, starting today, to change that pattern of behavior.

Action Steps

1. Focus on performing one task at a time for short periods. The goal is to develop a new habit to replace that of multitasking.

   It's not as easy as it sounds. If you're accustomed to doing multiple things at once, the practice of focusing on just one is likely to feel uncomfortable. That's the reason I suggest starting with short periods - for example, 10 minutes. Once you're able to focus for that long without problems, try 15 minutes. Then, 20 minutes.

   It's like starting an exercise program after years of leading a sedentary life. Start slowly. Think of this Action Step as a method of gradually building your single-tasking muscles.

2. Set aside your gadgets. Your phone, tablet and Apple Watch are digital enablers; they encourage you to multitask. How many times have you witnessed people playing with their phones, checking email and "Googling" information, while driving or holding a conversation?

   While you're working, turn off your phone and put it away. Do the same with your other devices. Keep them out of sight and out of reach and you'll be less drawn to them.

3. Commit to finishing the task at hand before addressing the next item on your to-do list. This step is a form of training. You're disciplining yourself to resist the temptation to tackle whatever happens to cross your desk.

   A quick side note: it won't always be possible to finish the task you've started. For example, suppose you need to obtain information from a coworker before you can move your project forward. With sound task management, you can mitigate this inconvenience.

   Continue working on the task at hand until you can go no further. Then, submit your request for information and choose another task to work on. When you receive the input you need, set it aside so you can leverage your momentum on the current task. Once you've completed it, resume work on the *first* task.

4. Create simple to-do lists. In Day 3, we discussed the value of keeping your to-do lists short and simple. Doing so will be an important part of breaking your multitasking habit.

   When you have a clear, prioritized list of items in front of you, it's easier to pick one and focus on it. Conversely, working without a to-do list, or working with one that is both complicated and overly-ambitious, increases the chances you'll attempt to address more than one item at a time.

5. Minimize interruptions. Your ability to concentrate will be crucial to developing the single-tasking habit. To that end, take steps to insulate yourself from incoming emails, phone calls, voicemails and texts. All of them will distract you, making it more difficult to focus.

Close your email and turn off your phone. Also, program your phone so it doesn't issue audible alerts when new emails or calls come in.

6. Declutter your desk. A messy desk will make you more inclined to multitask. It encourages your brain to flit from one item to the next. Clear your desk's surface of everything except the items you need to finish the task in front of you.

You don't have to organize your desk. Just put unnecessary items someplace out of sight. For example, throw them into a box for now. Organize them when you take a break or after you've completed the task at hand.

Day 17

Stop Refusing To
Take Responsibility For Your Choices

" If you could kick the person in the pants responsible for most of your trouble, you wouldn't sit for a month." - Theodore Roosevelt

We have a tendency to avoid taking responsibility for our actions and decisions. That's especially true if those actions and decisions have less-than-ideal outcomes.

It's human nature. Owning our decisions often forces us to face unpleasant consequences. So we avoid taking ownership.

For example, suppose you cause a car accident. Accepting responsibility for the mistakes that led to the accident would probably lead to higher insurance premiums.

Or suppose you're shopping in a store and inadvertently break something. Accepting blame might involve having to pay for the broken item.

Or suppose you're visiting Starbucks and drop your drink on the floor. Although you'll receive a free replacement drink, you'll still have to admit clumsiness.

Most of us are adverse to facing the music. So we naturally look for ways to avoid doing so.

The inclination to avoid owning our actions and decisions starts at an early age. We learn as children that staying silent when blame is assigned often allows us to sidestep repercussions. That tendency is reinforced through repeated application as we transition to adulthood.

But evading responsibility comes at a steep cost. The more often we do it, the more we convince ourselves that we have limited influence over outcomes.

That perspective leads to apathy. We start to see ourselves as victims of our circumstances rather than arbiters of our fate. We begin to believe that delusion. Mistakes and poor work processes aren't our fault, so there's nothing we can do to make notable improvements. We're not in control, so why bother trying to make things better?

If you don't see yourself as the captain of your ship, you'll be less inclined to change how you approach your workday. What would be the point?

Hopefully, you can see how that perspective can negatively impact your productivity.

How This Bad Habit Hurts Your Productivity

Refusing to take responsibility for our choices weakens our ability to work efficiently and effectively in five ways.

First, as noted above, it dampens our motivation and enthusiasm to make changes. We begin to assume our current workflow processes, some of which are unproductive, are a result of circumstance rather than personal choice. We feel we have no control over our workday, and thus any changes we might make would be a waste of time.

Second, it causes us to relegate ourselves to being just a cog or pawn, impotent and vulnerable to our environment and others' whims. We feel burdened with our work-related responsibilities while receiving little joy from our accomplishments. This can lead to increased stress, lower morale and eventually burnout.

Third, we lose the inspiration to produce high-quality work. Because we assume we have little to no influence over our circumstances, we see little value in expending time and effort to perform at a high level. So we spend our time producing mediocre work. Without inspiration, and in the absence of motivation and enthusiasm, we have little impetus to do otherwise.

Fourth, we're less motivated to take on challenging projects. Such projects carry a risk of failure. With failure comes the specter of consequences.

Such projects also carry the "risk" of success. With success comes the possibility that we'll be assigned more challenging projects. We're thus unmotivated to improve our productivity since doing so might result in unwanted - albeit positive - attention.

Fifth, our aversion to taking responsibility ultimately causes our careers to stall and our income to decline. We become predisposed to passing on opportunities that might otherwise lead to professional and personal growth.

The above side effects can have serious, lasting impacts on the amount of work you complete as well as the quality of that work. For that reason, it's worth developing the habit of owning your decisions and actions.

Action Steps

1. Assess how your workflow affects your goals. Think about how your actions lead to specific outcomes.

    For example, suppose your goal is to write a novel. You know intuitively that you must devote a significant amount of time, with your backside in a chair, to complete it. Unless you sit and write, your novel will never get finished. Unless you write productively, your novel will take *too long* to finish. You probably know people who have been writing their books for years.

The first step toward owning your decisions and actions is to consider how they influence outcomes. That will provide the motivation to make positive changes.

2. Ask yourself why you're inclined to avoid taking responsibility. As noted above, we learn the habit early in life. By the time we reach adulthood, it's ingrained in our minds. It becomes a pattern of behavior - one we rarely, if ever, analyze to determine its root causes.

But identifying the underlying reasons for this behavior is the key to changing it. Only then can we know where to focus our efforts in developing new, healthier habits.

Ask yourself whether you fear failure. Or like many people, do you fear success? Are you avoiding responsibility out of laziness? Each of these circumstances requires a different approach to effect a new habit.

3. Reframe mistakes as feedback. Too often, we regard mistakes as signs of failure. We assume they reflect a lack of competence and ability. We see feedback as a negative statement regarding our worth. It's no wonder so many of us develop a pattern of eschewing responsibility!

Undesired outcomes that stem from our mistakes merely inform us that, like everyone, we're imperfect. Importantly, they reveal areas for improvement. They do *not* signify a value statement about the individual.

Rather than reacting to your mistake with the question "Why do I always do the wrong thing?" ask yourself "What can I learn from this experience?"

4. Identify how fear affects you. Our tendency to avoid taking responsibility for our decisions and actions stems from fear. Fear of failure. Fear of success. Fear of the unknown. With rare exception, the fear is unfounded. Our minds exaggerate the potential for - and severity of - negative consequences.

   For example, suppose you're thinking about asking your employer for a raise. Your brain might suggest that you could be fired for having the audacity to do so (fear of failure). Or it may try to convince you that you'll be saddled with an unmanageable mountain of additional responsibilities along with the raise (fear of success).

   In reality, neither event is likely to happen.

   That's the reason it's important to identify how fear affects you. Once you're aware of how it exploits false impressions to maintain its power, you'll feel more confident in ignoring it.

5. Admit your mistakes with the intention of making improvements to your work habits. For example, if you know your procrastination resulted in a project being turned in late, own it. If you discover that your "open door" policy resulted in repeated interruptions that hampered your ability to get things done, accept responsibility for your decision.

   Then, make changes to avoid those problems in the future.

   Expect this Action Step to take time. Remember, you've spent a lifetime learning how to avoid taking responsibility for your decisions and actions to evade unpleasant consequences. It will take time to undo that pattern of behavior and replace it with a new, healthier and more productive habit.

Be patient with yourself.

Day 18

Stop Telling Yourself You're Not Ready

As we noted yesterday, we fear the unknown. For example, in our personal lives, we hesitate before saying hello to strangers. We immediately call a plumber before trying to fix plumbing problems on our own. We stick to the same grocery stores rather than visiting new stores. We gravitate toward the familiar.

In our professional lives, we shy away from taking on unfamiliar projects. We cringe at the thought of creating new spreadsheets and reports for our bosses. We balk at branching out into new avenues of business.

Instead, we remain in our comfort zones. There, after all, the risk of failure is minimal.

One of the biggest reasons we do this is because we believe we're unready to tackle new activities. We feel we lack the practical expertise to handle new projects with poise and effectiveness. We feel we lack the knowledge to know what we're doing. In other words, we tell ourselves that we're not 100% ready.

This assumption stems from a basic and common fallacy: that we must be 100% prepared if we hope to perform a given task effectively. In reality, that's untrue. The truth is, you'll rarely be 100% ready for anything life throws at you. Individuals who have achieved success in their respective fields claim their success is a reflection of their persistence and grit, and an ability to adapt to their circumstances. It is not dictated by whether the individual has achieved mastery in any particular area.

The reasons vary concerning why we tell ourselves we're not ready for a given task or assignment. For some of us, the hesitance to act stems from past failures that have had a significant impact on our self-confidence. We fear a repeat of those experiences. For others, the tendency toward inaction stems from an aversion to struggle. They consider every struggle toward a desired outcome as evidence of a lack of competence or preparation (or both).

In the next section, we'll explore how the habit of telling yourself you're not ready can have a negative impact on your productivity.

How This Bad Habit Hurts Your Productivity

First, you become less likely to take risks. Consequently, you're prevented from enjoying the rewards that come with taking those risks. Instead, you'll be inclined to stick to tasks and projects that allow you to stay within your comfort zone. They're "safe." They don't require you to wonder what might happen during the course of working on them.

Second, waiting until you're 100% ready - which is to say, never taking action - prevents you from expanding your areas of competency. Because you choose to stay within your comfort zone, you confront few challenges. As such, you're never faced with a problem that spurs you to broaden your skill set.

A third way this habit affects your productivity is that it encourages you to procrastinate. By convincing yourself you're not ready to undertake a given task, you'll find it's easier to rationalize postponing taking action. You'll start to spend an inordinate amount of time planning and preparing.

Fourth, staying in your comfort zone robs you of opportunities to impress influencers. After all, you're taking fewer risks. That means you'll rarely have a chance to stand apart from the pack.

Instead, you'll devote yourself to safe tasks and projects, which cause you to blend in with everyone else.

Fifth, constantly telling yourself you're not ready gradually erodes your self-confidence and morale. Over the long run, that diminishes your ability to work productively while increasing your stress levels.

The good news is that you can break this subversive habit and start enjoying the fruits of improved productivity. Following are seven ideas for making that happen.

Action Steps

1. Audit your current skill set. You have more areas of competence than you think.

   Throughout your life, you have amassed knowledge and specialized skills in a wide range of disciplines. That knowledge and those skills can prove useful to you in future endeavors.

   For example, I have a degree in Finance and Investments. Upon graduating from college, I accepted an accounting position with one of the top automakers. I then became a stockbroker. Then, I moved into a career in IT. For the past 20 years, I've been a writer in numerous capacities. Along the way, I learned about server management, Wordpress development and search engine optimization. All of these ventures imbued me with skills I use every day - in my business and personal life.

   Your experience has likewise instilled within you a raft of specialized skills. Many of them will help you to tackle unfamiliar tasks and projects, even if they seem unrelated to your current and previous jobs.

2. Focus on your desired outcomes rather than the things that might go wrong along the way.

One of our survival instincts is to plan for things that might go wrong. In some circumstances, that's a valuable quality that protects us from harm. It prevents us from strolling down dark alleys in unpopulated locales. It discourages us from petting strange dogs.

In other circumstances, however, it can hold us back. The instinct prevents us from pursuing opportunities that can lead to improved aptitude as well as personal and professional growth.

By focusing on your desire outcomes, you'll find it easier to ignore your inborn fear of the unknown. You'll be able to dismiss the voice in your head constantly whispering "What if XYZ happens?"

3. Look for opportunities to learn new skills. The self-confidence you'll gain will make you less fearful of tackling unfamiliar tasks.

Achieving a high level of competency in any discipline requires repeated exposure and application. There's no other way to attain proficiency. The problem is a lack of courage. It's normal to feel hesitant, or even intimidated, when we're given a new responsibility.

One way to boost your courage is to add to your overall skill set. Newly-learned skills don't have to be related to the unfamiliar task in front of you in order to offer value. The mere act of becoming proficient in them will give you more confidence in everything you do.

For example, many years ago, I learned how to code web pages using HTML and PHP. Learning those languages gave me the confidence to learn the basics of server management. One had nothing to do with the other. But I now had the *confidence* to learn to do the latter effectively. Had I not pushed myself to learn HTML and PHP, I would have avoided learning how to manage a server. I would have felt unready and fearful of failure.

Constantly broaden your skill set. You'll benefit from increased confidence that will give you the courage to take on - and even volunteer for - new projects.

4. Remind yourself that you'll never be 100% ready. Recognize it as an excuse your brain uses to discourage you from taking action.

5. Abandon the fear of others' criticism. One of the reasons we tell ourselves we're not ready to undertake a given task is because we're concerned what others will think if we fail.

Let go of that fear. Realize that others' perceptions of us are often inaccurate. They don't know our circumstances. They're not privy to our goals. And often, their negativity is a reflection of their own perceived limitations. They have nothing to do with you.

Don't let others' criticism stop you from tackling unfamiliar tasks and moving them forward.

6. Remind yourself that undesired outcomes are merely feedback. They're not statements regarding your competence. They reflect problems in your decision-making or work processes, or both. To that end, they present opportunities to improve.

We learn more from our mistakes than we do from our successes. Indeed, our mistakes are among our most valuable learning tools.

7. Develop the habit of taking action, even when tasks and projects are not completely planned out.

The only way to become more comfortable with venturing outside your comfort zone is to do so on a repeated basis. Look for opportunities to perform activities and take on projects that are new to you.

Accept in advance that your results might fail to meet your expectations. The object is to develop a new habit that eliminates your fear of the unknown, not to master a particular skill or effect an ideal outcome.

Day 19

Stop Neglecting To Organize Your Day

Staying organized is a crucial part of effective time management. It allows you to stay focused and work efficiently. It helps you to ignore distractions and get into a state of flow.

Poor organization has the opposite effects, and can thus impede your productivity. For example, if you work without a to-do list or spend the day reacting to others' last-minute demands, you'll find it difficult to get things done. Or if your desk is cluttered, you'll be more susceptible to distractions. That alone can lead to an array of negative effects on your ability to get things done (we'll discuss these in the following section).

The causal relationship between disorganization and diminished productivity is universal; it affects everyone. It also has scientific support. In 2011, the Journal of Neuroscience published a study examining the cognitive effects of clutter, a common sign of general disorganization. The authors found that clutter impairs our ability to concentrate and process new information.

It's clear that being organized helps your productivity. But it may be less clear whether you're working in that state. If you lack the benefit of ongoing feedback concerning your efficiency, you might assume your workflow is fine. This is common with people who work from home (I speak from experience). They have the freedom to work at their own pace. Lacking a feedback loop, they never realize how inefficient their work processes are.

How do you know if you need to make changes to your workflow? Signs of a problem include working without a schedule, working without a to-do list and working on a cluttered desk.

Other signs are subtler. For example, do you know which of the day's tasks are high priorities and which can be postponed or eliminated? If not, you can benefit from better organization. Are you frequently interrupted or distracted? If so, your day might need more structure.

In a moment, I'll give you several ideas that will help you to become more organized. First, let's take a closer look at the ways disorganization hobbles your ability to work productively.

How This Bad Habit Hurts Your Productivity

Disorganization, in all its many forms, may seem harmless in the moment, especially if you've grown accustomed to it. For example, if your desk has always been cluttered, you might not realize the extent to which clutter impacts your ability to work. In truth, being disorganized lessens your productivity in seven ways.

First, it hampers your ability to focus. You're less able to concentrate on the task in front of you. That forces you to take more time than necessary to complete it.

Second, you become more prone to distractions. Without the benefit of a concrete schedule of time blocks and breaks, guided by a clearly-defined to-do list, boredom is likely to set in. That makes you more vulnerable to the siren call of social media, email and other diversions.

Third, being disorganized makes you more receptive to interruptions. When you work without a schedule or to-do list, there's a lesser sense of urgency. Consequently, there's a lower perceived need to drive off coworkers, friends and family members (if you work from home) who visit your office or cubicle.

Fourth, distractions and interruptions carry a switching cost. I mentioned this in previous chapters (e.g. Days 1, 12 and 16). Each time you switch from one task to another, you lose momentum. Lost momentum takes at least 20 minutes to regain. The more complex the tasks, the greater the setback in terms of time lost.

Fifth, when you're disorganized and prone to distractions, you're unable to achieve a flow state. Flow is being "in the zone." It's a state of consciousness in which you're completely focused on the task in front of you. When you're in a flow state, you're more creative and productive. You're also able to process information more effectively.

Sixth, disorganization robs you of control over your day. Because you're constantly distracted and vulnerable to interruptions, your workday is spent reacting to external stimuli. You waste precious time on Facebook and Twitter. You accept calls from friends and family members. You give full attention to coworkers who drop by your office to chat. As a result, you never truly hold the reins over your workday.

Seventh, you experience more stress. The brain prefers structure. It favors organization. When you're disorganized, you're unable to relax because you feel as if your work is never done. The constant feeling that you've left work unfinished leads to guilt and anxiety.

In short, mess causes stress.

If your typical workday is mired in chaos, the seven negative effects above should motivate you to make changes. Here are seven ideas for giving your day more structure and thereby boosting your productivity.

Action Steps

1. Create simple, goal-oriented to-do lists. We covered how to create effective to-do lists in Day 3. The key here is twofold. First, limit your lists to five items. The shorter, the better. Second, eliminate any tasks that fail to align with your goals.

   Also, create your to-do lists the night before. Don't wait until you arrive at your office to do so. Arriving prepared will help you to start the day feeling organized.

2. Use time blocks or the Pomodoro Technique to schedule work sessions and breaks. Resist the temptation to deviate from your schedule, even if you achieve a flow state. It's more important to develop the habit of staying organized and on task.

   If you work in a corporate environment, print your schedule and display it where others can see it. That way, if coworkers visit to chat, you can refer to your schedule and ask them to come back later.

   If you work at home or a coffee shop, have your schedule nearby. That way, it will serve as a constant reminder of the times during which you should be working.

3. Create time blocks for addressing others' demands. People are going to interrupt you, especially in the beginning when you're developing this new habit. At that point, you haven't yet set the expectation that you're unreceptive to their impromptu visits. Now's the time to "train" them.

   Set aside 30 minutes in the afternoon to follow up with people who asked for your attention earlier in the day. By handling their requests in a single 30-minute window, you'll avoid forfeiting your momentum to a string of midday interruptions.

Schedule the time block toward the end of the day when your energy is waning. Then, tell anyone who visits that you'll be happy to help them during your regularly-scheduled 30-minute time block.

4. Schedule your work sessions and breaks according to the times of day you have the most energy.

   Your energy levels directly impact your productivity. Don't fight it. If you do your best work between 7:00 a.m. and noon, build your schedule around that personal sweet spot. Focus on complex tasks in the morning and leave dull tasks for the afternoon. If your energy is highest between 1:00 p.m. and 6:00 p.m., schedule your work sessions and breaks accordingly.

5. Track your time. If you're disorganized, you're allowing time to slip through your fingers. Tracking how you use your time will reveal ways in which you can improve.

   You might be surprised by the results. For example, you may find you're spending far more time than you realized on social media. Or you might discover that coworkers' interruptions are costing you two hours in lost time each day.

   Famous management consultant Peter Drucker used to say "what gets measured gets improved." To that end, use tools like Toggl or RescueTime to measure how you use your time. Track your usage and record the results for two weeks to identify unproductive trends.

6. Say "no" to impromptu meetings. Just because there's something to discuss doesn't mean it must be discussed at that moment. Most items can wait.

If you work in an office and your coworkers want to have an unplanned meeting, decline the request. Suggest a later time, either that day or later in the week.

Do likewise if you're self-employed and a client requests an impromptu meeting. Rather than agreeing to meet at that moment, even on the phone, suggest a later time. That will help you to keep your day organized.

7. Limit meetings to 10 minutes. And prohibit the use of chairs.

Most meetings take more time than necessary. Part of the reason is because too much time is allocated for them. If an hour is set aside for a meeting, the meeting is likely to take the entire hour. Allocating 10 minutes gives participants a sense of urgency.

Parkinson's Law states that "work expands so as to fill the time available for its completion." So it is with meetings.

Another reason meetings go on too long is because the participants are comfortably seated. So remove the chairs. Those in attendance will be more inclined to finish the meeting early and return to their offices and cubicles, where their comfy chairs are waiting for them.

Day 20

Stop Feeling Sorry For Yourself

" Self-pity is easily the most destructive of the non-pharmaceutical narcotics; it is addictive, gives momentary pleasure and separates the victim from reality." - John Gardner, Secretary of Health, Education and Welfare under President Lyndon Johnson

Bad things happen to all of us. How we respond to such things defines us and dictates our effectiveness in everything we do.

Many people respond to unpleasant circumstances by feeling sorry for themselves. Doing so gives them comfort. It also provides a source of attention and validation from others, both of which fill the gap left by a low self-image.

Others respond by taking steps to learn from their mistakes (if any) and change their situation. Rather than feeling sorry for themselves, they try to determine the cause of their misfortune so they can enjoy better results down the road. Then, they formulate a plan for rising above their current state.

For example, suppose you lose your job. You have two options. First, you can lament your situation and cry "why do these things always happen to me?" Or you could evaluate the reasons you lost your job. That way, you can improve areas in your professional life in which you're lacking. Then, start looking for a new position.

The latter approach gives you more control over your life. While self-pity turns you into a (self-perceived) victim of fate, embracing your personal responsibility and making positive changes puts you in the driver's seat.

Are you inclined to feel sorry for yourself when things don't go your way? Do you secretly hope things go wrong because you know others will pay attention to you? Have you ever said to yourself that life is unfair?

If so, you're allowing self-pity to hold you back. It's preventing you from accomplishing your goals, including maintaining a high level of productivity - both in your personal and professional life.

How This Bad Habit Hurts Your Productivity

A victim mentality - the tendency to feel sorry for yourself - hinders your productivity in four ways. First, when you view everything through the lens of how life is unfair, you learn to never take responsibility for your actions and decisions. That gives you implicit permission to blame others for your misfortune. Consequently, you never take the time to improve your work habits because you see yourself as never being in control. (We discussed this false chain of reasoning in Day 17).

Second, wallowing in self-pity sets the stage for discouragement and depression. It may initially feel good since it attracts attention and validation from others. But it reinforces the false notion that you are a victim of circumstance. You eventually convince yourself that you're a magnet for adversity with no means to avoid it.

Third, it stunts your self-confidence. You begin to see yourself as being unable to overcome obstacles or work in a manner that prevents them. As a result, you become averse to risk, preferring instead to stay within your comfort zone. That ultimately curbs your professional and personal growth. You're left working on the same mundane tasks day after day, leading to boredom and stress, and increasing the risk of burnout.

Fourth, self-pity is self-perpetuating. The more you hold onto it, the more it festers and becomes part of your identity. It eventually informs every decision you make.

There's a better way. Here are eight action steps to help you abandon the tendency toward self-pity and reclaim the reins of your productivity.

Action Steps

1. Identify actions that indicate a penchant for self-pity. Once you recognize them, you can actively short-circuit them and break the pattern of feeling sorry for yourself.

    Our actions condition us. They form self-reinforcing patterns of behavior. And the more often they're expressed, the more ingrained they become as habits. This Action Step attempts to wear down the pattern of self-pity and lay the groundwork for developing better habits in its place.

2. Acknowledge your role in making decisions and taking actions that lead to unpleasant situations. Take personal responsibility for your circumstances. We covered this in detail in Day 17.

    For example, suppose your auto insurer raises your premiums after you receive a number of speeding tickets. Rather than seeing yourself as a hapless victim of your insurer's greed, acknowledge that you chose, more than once, to break the speed limit.

    Once you own your decisions and actions, you'll be empowered to make changes that can effect better outcomes.

3. Create a list of things for which you're grateful. Place it somewhere within your reach, such as in front of your computer. When you start to feel like a victim of circumstance, review the list to remind yourself of your good fortune.

   Gratitude is the sworn enemy of self-pity. When you reflect on the things that make your life better - for example, a roof over your head, food on your table and a loving family - you become less inclined to feel sorry for yourself.

4. Create a list of things you can change or influence. It will contradict your penchant for feeling like a victim. When you notice the first signs of self-pity, review the list to remind yourself of the level of influence you wield.

   Your list will be longer than you imagine. That's the reason to create it.

   The types of items you add to your list will depend on your circumstances. For example, if you're a financial planner, you dictate your level of professionalism and breadth of knowledge about various investment vehicles. If you're a freelance web designer, you influence your rates and whether you turn in projects on time. If you're a college student, you determine the amount of time you spend studying for exams.

   Once you recognize how much influence you have over your circumstances, you can dismantle the victim mentality that plagues you.

5. Realize that life isn't fair. One of the reasons people feel sorry for themselves is because they feel they're not given the same opportunities as others. But that perception is based on the fallacy that life should be equitable for everyone.

Life isn't fair. Some people are born to riches while others are born in abject poverty. Some people seem naturally talented at everything they do while others seem hopelessly inept. Let go of the notion that life should be fair.

6. Instead of assigning blame for undesired outcomes, look for opportunities to make a positive change in your life. It's by evaluating our lives and making calculated changes that we improve our circumstances.

When something goes wrong in your life, resist the temptation to point your finger at another person. Instead, consider how your actions may have contributed to your current predicament. Then, brainstorm ways to do things differently next time.

7. Stop comparing yourself to other people.

Self-pity needs a baseline. It needs a yardstick. Otherwise, it has no power.

For example, you might feel sorry for yourself because your neighbor has a larger home than you. Or your coworker received a larger raise than you. Or your friend's children are better-behaved than your children.

Stop focusing on others' advantages in life. There is no way to know their circumstances. Moreover, by breaking the habit, you'll dilute the power of self-pity and feel less a victim.

8. Improve your self-esteem. Have confidence in your skills and knowledge. That confidence will serve as a barrier against self-pity.

How do you build self-esteem? Following are a few ideas you can take action on immediately:

- Take on a new hobby, ideally one that encourages you to spend time with other people.
- Start exercising and following a healthy diet.
- Remind yourself of your core competencies are areas of expertise.
- Volunteer for charity work.
- Pick a new skill and learn to master it.
- Silence your inner critic.
- Acknowledge mistakes with the intention of improving yourself.
- Smile at strangers.

There are hundreds, if not thousands, of simple ways you can improve your self-esteem. Pick a few and watch how they boost your confidence and improve your outlook on life. Then, watch as your new confidence and outlook stimulate your productivity.

Day 21

Stop Working Against
Your Body's Natural Rhythm

Your productivity is influenced by your energy levels. Those levels rise and fall based on your body's natural rhythm. Accommodate that rhythm and you'll be able to work faster with fewer errors. Ignore it and you'll end up spinning your wheels and making little progress on your to-do list.

There are two types of natural body rhythms. The first type is known as a circadian rhythm. It defines the body's 24-hour cycle. Specifically, it explains the effect of light and darkness in the natural environment on our brain wave activity, physiology and behavior.

Put simply, it's our biological "clock."

The circadian rhythm influences your energy levels, and thus determines when you're likely to be most and least productive during a given 24-hour cycle. As such, you can optimize your productivity by scheduling certain types of tasks during certain times of the day. For example, work on difficult tasks when your energy level is high and simple tasks when your energy level is low.

The second type of natural body rhythm is known as an ultradian rhythm. During a single circadian day (24 hours), your body goes through a series of shorter cycles. Each one lasts between 90 and 120 minutes. Your level of alertness changes during these cycles.

Have you ever wondered why you experience a mental lull after 90 minutes of focused work? The lull is due to your ultradian rhythm.

Most people ignore their bodies' rhythms. They blast through their work when their energy levels are high and press on when their energy levels are low. It's a noble attempt to get as much done as possible. But it's one that ultimately does more harm than good. Their productivity suffers from the law of diminishing marginal returns. The longer they press on, the less effective and efficient they become.

Your goal should be to identify when your energy levels are at their peak and at their minimum, and schedule your day accordingly. Monotonous tasks like email can be done when your energy is low. Creative tasks like writing an article for publication should be done when your energy is high.

It's not easy to align your workflow with your circadian and ultradian rhythms. But doing so is definitely worth the effort. Ignoring your body's natural cycles can cripple your ability to get things done in a reasonable time frame.

How This Bad Habit Hurts Your Productivity

Working against your natural rhythms is a bad idea for five reasons. First, you'll end up wasting peak-alertness time on mundane tasks. Consequently, you'll be left to address complex tasks when your mental resources are on the wane.

For example, suppose normally you respond to emails between 10:00 a.m. and noon, a period during which you feel energized and alert. That's a waste of mental energy. Email doesn't require significant cognitive resources. It can be done effectively when your energy level is low, such as the hour immediately following lunch.

A second consequence of ignoring your body's rhythms is that you'll end up spending too much time working on complex tasks. Because you'll often be addressing such tasks when your energy level is low, you'll be less able to focus on them. That will hamper your ability to work efficiently.

Third, your motivation will suffer a blow. As you force yourself to work through periods of low energy, you'll feel as if you're progressing at a snail's pace. You'll sense that your output isn't commensurate with your effort.

Fourth, you'll find it increasingly difficult to concentrate on difficult tasks. As your energy and alertness decline, your ability to focus will deteriorate.

Fifth, disregarding your circadian and ultradian rhythms makes you more vulnerable to distractions. The less you're able to concentrate on your work, the more inclined you'll be to look for diversions.

Let's work on getting your day back on track. Here are six action steps that will help you to leverage your energy levels and thereby boost your productivity.

Action Steps

1. Track your energy levels and ability to focus for two weeks. Assign both aspects a value between one and ten. A value of one signifies low energy or an inability to concentrate. A value of ten signifies high energy or sharp focus. Monitor both on an hourly basis. Write the values down or enter them into a spreadsheet so you can review them later.

   It's a good idea to limit the amount of caffeine and other stimulants you use to boost your energy and level of alertness. Doing so will allow you to track fluctuations in both with a higher degree of accuracy.

2. Create a list of tasks you perform on a regular basis. Separate them into three groups according to their level of complexity.

For example, sending emails, returning calls and inputting data should be placed in the "simple tasks" group. Writing articles, analyzing data and creating marketing campaigns should be categorized as "complex" tasks. They require considerable thought. Other activities, such as negotiating terms with vendors or creating goals for the coming year, fall somewhere in the middle. They should be designated "medium complexity" tasks.

3. Pinpoint the time of day during which you typically have the most energy. That's when you should tackle your most complex assignments.

   This step is an extension of Action Step #1. After tracking changes in your energy levels and ability to concentrate for two weeks, you'll see noticeable trends. You'll observe the times during which you're able to work at peak productivity. Leverage that part of your day to work on high-value tasks that require your concentration.

4. Identify your lowest-energy time of day. That's when you should work on tedious, low-value tasks. Or take a 30-minute nap. When you awake, you'll feel refreshed and be able to take full advantage of your next ultradian rhythm.

5. Note how your diet affects your energy level. How do you feel after eating a nutritious breakfast? Is your energy level high or low? Do you feel invigorated or lethargic?

   Likewise, how do you feel after eating junk food (ice cream, candy bars, etc.)? Does the sugar rush give you a burst of energy that quickly evaporates and leaves you feeling sluggish?

   Track how your mind and body react to the foods you eat. Then, adjust your diet to optimize your ability to focus and get things done.

6. Leverage the two hours before lunch. That's when you're likely to be at peak alertness. If you're like most people, that will be the best time to address your most complex assignments. But track your energy levels and ability to focus for at least two weeks to make certain.

Day 22

Stop Refusing To Get Enough Exercise

❝ If I knew I was going to live this long, I'd have taken better care of myself." - baseball legend Mickey Mantle

Regardless of your job title, your goal should be to increase your productivity in any way you can. Working faster means getting more things done and enjoying more free time. That can open the door to an array of rewarding benefits, such as spending more time with your family, having the opportunity to start a side business or impressing your boss and receiving a raise.

For that reason, it's worth doing everything you can to improve the efficiency of your workflow.

That includes getting regular exercise.

Research shows that staying fit has a positive effect on cognitive ability and productivity. In one study, published in the Proceedings of the National Academy of Sciences in 2011, researchers found that moderate exercise improved spatial memory in older adults.

In another study, researchers provided treadmill desks to the employees of a Minnesota loan company. The desks forced the employees to walk and work at the same time. The researchers found that the staff's performance improved significantly compared to their performance while sitting at their desks. The findings were published in the journal PLOS One in 2013.

There are many benefits associated with exercise. They include less stress, improved memory, better focus, better mood, increased alertness, heightened brain function and more creativity. Studies also show that people who regularly exercise are more likely than their sedentary counterparts to enjoy a more positive work-life balance.

Most people get too little exercise. They sit in front of their computers for most of the workday and sit on their couches for most of the evening. Consequently, they never give themselves the opportunity to enjoy the benefits of physical exertion.

Reasons vary. We tell ourselves that we lack the time to go to the gym or are unable to afford a gym membership. Or we find exercise boring. Or we don't know how to do it properly. Or we have to watch our kids and are thus unable to get to the gym. Or we simply hate exercise.

Most reasons are little more than excuses. They rationalize inaction. And they weaken more than just your body; they undermine your productivity.

How This Bad Habit Hurts Your Productivity

A sedentary lifestyle impairs your ability to get things done in eight distinct ways. First, it makes you more vulnerable to stress. Regardless of whether you work in a corporate office or at home, stress is an ever-present part of your day. It's often subtle and difficult to recognize, but it's always there.

Exercise releases endorphins that lessen the toll stress takes on you. Without it, stress can build to the point that it severely harms your performance at work.

Second, neglecting to exercise sets the stage for lagging energy levels. When you work out, your body is better able to metabolize glucose, delivering it to your brain and the rest of your body. The glucose gives you energy.

When you sit in front of your computer all day, you don't enjoy that effect. Your body can still metabolize glucose and send it to your brain, but it does so less efficiently.

Third, a sedentary lifestyle diminishes your focus and level of alertness. Blood flow to the brain is less robust than would be the case if you followed a regular exercise regimen.

Fourth, lack of exercise can cause weight gain and lead to obesity. That, in turn, can open the door to serious health issues, such as metabolic syndrome and type 2 diabetes. Such problems make it more difficult to work productively since you often feel in poor health.

A fifth side effect of sedentary behavior is the erosion of memory and cognitive skills. Research shows that the prefrontal cortex, the part of the brain that influences memory and information processing, is smaller in individuals who neglect to exercise.

Sixth, you're more likely to sleep poorly. In 2013, The National Sleep Foundation polled 1,000 adults aged between 23 and 60. The organization found that people who regularly exercised were far more likely to report getting a good night's sleep than those who didn't exercise. Vigorous exercisers enjoyed the best sleep. They also reported the fewest sleep problems.

Seventh, you're more likely to be irritable. Studies have shown a causal connection between a sedentary lifestyle and anxiety and depression. Both latter attributes can make you short-tempered with your coworkers, friends and family members.

Lastly, a lack of exercise is likely to negatively affect your work-life balance. Researchers have found that people who exercise on a regular basis are better able to manage their time and handle the demands associated with their responsibilities.

Let's assume you currently get little to no exercise. Following are seven suggestions for improving that area of your life and giving your productivity a healthy boost in the process. (If you regularly work out, feel free to skip the following section.)

Action Steps

1. Clean up your diet. We talked about diet in Day 9. It's a crucial first step to getting into shape. An exercise regimen married to a terrible diet will have a limited impact on your productivity. Moreover, eating unhealthy foods will lessen your motivation to get into shape.

2. Get sufficient sleep. It's important that you get seven to eight hours of sleep each night. Only then will you be able to sustain a regular exercise regimen. If you only sleep five hours a night, you will eventually feel run down. Naturally, your motivation to work out will wane.

3. Schedule time to exercise. Treat it like an appointment with yourself. Many people plan to work out, but fail to do so because "life" gets in their way. That includes their work responsibilities, time spent with family and going out with friends.

    These things are important, of course. But there's a way to manage all of them. It's a matter of prioritization. Make an appointment to exercise. Then, stick to it, just as you would with any work-related meeting.

4. Invest in a standing desk. It will encourage you to move your body throughout the workday.

    Research shows that sitting for several hours introduces a number of health risks. It can lead to muscle degeneration, neck and back pain and can even shorten your life. A standing desk gets you on your feet. It short circuits the physiological processes that make sitting unhealthy.

A quick tip: don't stand for several hours at a time. Doing so will do more harm than good. Instead, alternate. Stand for 60 minutes, then sit for 60 minutes, and then stand up again. It helps to use an adjustable-height standing desk that can be raised and lowered with the touch of a button. I use a Jarvis standing desk and love it.

5. Track where you're spending your time during the day. That will reveal short time blocks you can use to exercise.

   You don't need two hours to work out. The goal is to simply move your body, not sculpt it with chiseled muscles. You can do that in 5-minute increments. For example, if you're at the office, take a 5-minute break and perform a few stretches, squats and pushups. If you're at home, go for a short walk around the block.

   The purpose of tracking your time is to find pockets of "dead" time - five minutes here and ten minutes there - you can use to work your muscles and get your blood flowing.

6. Start slowly. If you've spent the last few years living a sedentary lifestyle, don't go for a 40-minute jog at the outset. Instead, start with a brisk 10-minute walk. Then, day by day, increase the duration of your walks to 15 minutes, then 20 minutes and then 25 minutes.

   After a week, advance to jogging, but only for short intervals. Jog for five minutes a day during the first week. Jog for ten minutes a day during the second week. Follow that pattern until you build the needed stamina and respiratory strength to safely jog for 40 minutes without rest.

Starting slowly gives you motivation to continue developing the habit of exercise. It also helps you to avoid hurting yourself.

7. Track your daily exercises on a spreadsheet. That way, you can monitor your progress. Over time, you'll see clear evidence of increasing strength and endurance, which will motivate you to continue.

Day 23

Stop Worrying About What Others Think Of You

" Do not fear to be eccentric in opinion, for every opinion now accepted was once eccentric." - Bertrand Russell

I'm guilty of it. You are, too.

We're hardwired to care what others think about us. The only exceptions are sociopaths.

We're born with the instinct, and both benefit from it and suffer its drawbacks. On the one hand, caring about others' opinions helps us to distinguish between behaviors that are appropriate and inappropriate. For example, if those nearby stand to their feet when an individual enters the room, we're inclined to follow suit. It's human nature.

On the other hand, seeking approval from others can hinder us from growing - both professionally and personally. For example, suppose you're in a meeting and your coworkers are hesitant to express their ideas. If you follow their lead, you'll remain silent and go unnoticed. If you give voice to your ideas - that is, you "go against the herd" - you'll gain the attention of the person (or persons) managing the meeting. Assuming your ideas are insightful, such attention could benefit your career.

Most of us spend a considerable portion of our waking hours worrying about whether our peers - coworkers, friends and family members - approve of our decisions and actions. In some cases, we aim to impress them. In other cases, we fear looking foolish or eccentric in front of them.

Unfortunately, doing so holds us back. Rather than taking risks in order to achieve our goals, we become more inclined to accept the status quo. Consequently, we inhibit our growth.

The Chinese philosopher Lao Tzu once said "care about what other people think and you will always be their prisoner." Reflect on times when you refused to act without the tacit approval of your peers. Chances are, you benefited little from your inaction. On the contrary, you probably missed out on valuable opportunities.

The first step toward change is to identify the level of influence others' opinions have over you. All of us suffer from this ingrained habit. But some of us do so to a much greater extent than others. It's important to know the extent to which this habit affects your life.

Ask yourself the following questions:

- Do I frequently remain closemouthed due to fear concerning what my peers might think of me?
- Do I often think people are angry with me when, in fact, they are not?
- Do I find myself doing things I dislike in order to gain the approval of friends and family members?
- Do I keep my distance from people who I suspect don't like me?
- Do I have trouble making decisions?

If you answered yes to any of the above questions, you're caught in a trap. You care too much about others' opinions about you, and are likely missing great opportunities to grow professionally and personally.

Today, your goal is to detach yourself from this self-sabotaging habit. Rather than seeking peer approval for your actions, decisions and ambitions, you'll develop confidence in yourself.

Before we get to today's action steps, let's talk briefly about how worrying about others' opinions diminishes your productivity.

How This Bad Habit Hurts Your Productivity

I've already mentioned some of the ways seeking others' approval for your decisions and actions can impede your growth. Let's revisit them in the context of how they compromise your ability to get things done.

First, concerning yourself about what others think makes you less likely to take risks and try new things. That, in turn, prevents you from expanding your knowledge, adding to your skill set and testing new ways to complete projects more efficiently. Instead, as noted above, you remain content with the status quo.

Second, you miss out on opportunities. Those opportunities might include receiving a promotion that allows you to delegate tasks to others. Or you might be given a chance to manage high-value projects with more exposure to senior staff members. That would allow you to see the bigger picture and make connections with people who can help your career. If you fail to act due to how you imagine others will perceive you, such opportunities might never surface.

Third, you start to feel resentment over missed opportunities. You're aware of the overt influence others' opinions have over you. You recognize that your concerns are holding you back. They're preventing you from enjoying the benefits of taking action. Being aware of that fact can cause you to begrudge your peers. It can even lead to self-loathing as you realize your timidity is impeding your growth.

Fourth, like all habits, the practice of seeking others' approval reinforces itself. It becomes more deeply rooted each time you do it.

As a result, you never manage to develop the confidence you need to act without first receiving validation from others. These side effects harm your ability to work productively. Your need for implicit approval trumps the motivation to proactively improve your work processes. Let's make a positive change. Here are seven action steps you can take, starting today, to break the habit.

Action Steps

1. Realize you're not everyone else's top priority. Chances are, most of the people you're worried about aren't devoting as much time and attention to your decisions as you imagine. As author David Foster Wallace once said, "You'll worry less about what people think about you when you realize how seldom they do."

2. Identify the people whose opinions *should* matter to you. For example, your boss's sentiments are likely more valuable than a coworker's who has no experience with the type of project you're working on.

3. Thicken your skin. Look for opportunities to attract feedback and criticism. For example, start a blog and express controversial opinions. Volunteer to speak in front of a tough audience.

At first, others' disapproval will seem jarring. It might even be heartbreaking. But the more disapproval you receive, the thicker your skin will grow. Eventually, you'll be able to dismiss others' opinions or grow from them.

Forming this habit takes time and repeated exposure. Keep in mind, consistent application is crucial when adopting any new behavioral pattern. So be patient with yourself.

4. Reevaluate your goals and their respective priorities in your life. Write them down in the order of their importance. This simple practice is often enough to put others' opinions in perspective.

   For example, suppose you want to start a business. It's a top priority in your life. Sadly, your friends don't support your aspirations. They believe you shouldn't waste your time since the failure rate with new businesses is so high.

   Write your goal of starting a business at the top of your list. Include a few notes concerning how you hope the new business will change your circumstances. With your goal listed prominently at the top of your list, you'll be less influenced by your friends' doom-and-gloom advice.

5. Identify three people who inspire you. Reflect on their lives whenever you face criticism - implicit or otherwise - from your peers.

   For example, one of my inspirations is Mahatma Gandhi. He received criticism and adversity from all corners. Yet, he pressed on, spurred by his convictions. When I confront others' disapproval, I reflect on Gandhi's life.

   Do likewise with your own collection of individuals who inspire you.

6. Realize criticism often reflects self-perceived deficits in the critic. Many people attack the ideas and decisions of others out of self-loathing or general unhappiness about their own lives. There is nothing you can do about that. Protect yourself and dismiss their opinions.

7. Remind yourself of the worst possible outcome of taking action. We often consider inaction to be safe and taking action to represent risk. If we act, bad things might happen.

But this fear is almost always misplaced. The worst case scenario that plays over and over in our minds is a gross exaggeration of reality. It is highly unlikely to come to pass. Don't let fear stop you from taking action. Get into the habit of ignoring it and pressing on according to your convictions.

Day 24

Stop Keeping Up With Current Events

" The man who reads nothing at all is better educated than the man who reads nothing but newspapers."
- Thomas Jefferson

Most of us are addicts.

We're addicted to news. As long as we get our regular fix, we can go about our day, comfortable in the knowledge that we're informed regarding current events. But if we erect a wall between ourselves and the never-ending news cycle, shunning our "drug" of choice, we experience withdrawals.

Like all addictions, an addiction to current events carries consequences. Those consequences adversely impact our lives in myriad ways.

For example, we train ourselves to consider news bulletins a high priority that supersede everything else. And the more we indulge our habit, the more we reinforce it. Eventually, we become obsessed, looking for a fix when we should be working on the tasks on our to-do lists.

It's worth noting that few events reported in the news have any real longevity. Incidents that seem significant in the moment are forgotten the following week. Within two or three months, few even warrant the smallest of footnotes. Given that fact, the attention devoted to them today is wasted.

Here's another problem: much of the news we see on television, the internet or in newspapers is shallow. The stories are little more than sound bytes designed to draw us in. They feed our craving for current events, but keep us wanting more. Some stories masquerade as news, but are intended to amuse rather than inform.

Comedian Jerry Seinfeld once said "It's amazing that the amount of news that happens in the world every day always just exactly fits the newspaper." He was kidding, of course. But his joke underscores the fact that news bulletins are seldom critical or deserving of our attention.

You might assume your fondness for current events has little to no impact on your productivity. In truth, it has a much bigger impact than you might realize.

How This Bad Habit Hurts Your Productivity

First, most news announcements are negative. You may have heard the saying "if it bleeds, it leads." That maxim reflects the news media's prioritization of stories depicting violence, misery and death. The idea is that people are drawn to gloomy narratives more than they are drawn to positive narratives.

The constant barrage of negativity makes you more passive. You become less likely to take action and less likely to look for ways to improve your circumstances. This effect can be seen with any type of passive entertainment. But it is especially prominent when it stems from an ongoing diet of negative, fear-based news.

A second consequence of this type of addiction is an increased susceptibility to distractions. Current events are delivered in seductive, sensational sound bytes aimed at pulling you in. They hint at juicy details that promise to sate your inner voyeur.

The result? The news items become irresistible.

Third, your heightened vulnerability to distractions destroys your focus. You're less able to concentrate on your work, and thus less able to work efficiently. In Day 12, we discussed the importance of momentum in your workflow. Each time your momentum is broken, you need 20 minutes to get back on track. Imagine how difficult it is to maintain a high level of productivity if you're constantly distracted by the siren call of current events.

Fourth, the more receptive you are to distractions, the more responsive you'll be to interruptions. You may even seek them out if you're bored.

Fifth, a news addiction can cause you to lose motivation that might otherwise inspire you to work more productively. How did you feel the last time you watched an hour of your favorite news program on television? Did you feel inspired to get things done? Did the stories and bulletins rouse you to manage your time more effectively? If you're like most people, they had the opposite effect. They drained your energy and made you feel lethargic. The constant negativity may have even caused you to feel depressed.

Let's assume you have a news addiction. You watch or read the news throughout the day to "stay informed." How do you overcome your habit?

Follow these six action steps.

Action Steps

1. Start a news fast. Refrain from watching news on television or reading it online. If you receive daily emails from your favorite news site (for example, CNN.com), unsubscribe. Otherwise, you'll be tempted to read them every time they arrive in your inbox.

I recommend continuing your fast for at least two weeks. Four weeks is better. That gives you enough time to break the habit and replace it with one that's healthier and more rewarding over the long run.

Fair warning: the first day of your fast will be difficult. You'll be tempted to cheat (e.g. "*I'll just check CNN this one time.*") Realize it gets easier with each passing day. The longer your fast continues, the more you'll feel in control of your addiction.

2. Write down a list of topics that interest you. For example, you might enjoy stories about technological breakthroughs. Or you might like news items regarding medical treatments for specific health conditions. Specify the types of announcements you have a particular interest in and only read those stories.

Doing so limits your consumption of news. It allows you to avoid useless news bulletins involving violence, misery and mayhem. Instead, you're able to focus your attention on the stories you enjoy, freeing up your time to get more work done.

3. Use Google Alerts to deliver a weekly digest of stories that address your interests. That eliminates the need to search for the topics you listed in Action Step #2. Your Alerts will notify you when news bulletins about them surface.

For example, suppose you want to stay informed about the latest pharmacologic cancer treatments. You could scour the medical sections of your favorite news websites each day, looking for relevant stories. Or simply create a Google Alert to do the heavy lifting for you. You'll receive short summaries of recently-published stories, along with links to where you can read them in their entirety, via email.

Not only does this save you time and effort, but it also helps you to break the habit of actively checking for the latest news bulletins.

4. Remove all bookmarks in your browser that point to your favorite news websites. Doing so will force you to type in the URLs for the sites you want to visit, which will dampen your motivation to visit them.

   The simple act of typing "NYTimes.com" or "CNN.com" into your browser may be enough to short-circuit the habit of checking for the latest headlines.

5. Brainstorm a short list of activities you can enjoy in the place of watching the news. This list will serve as a reminder of the activities you're choosing to forfeit for your news addiction.

   Your list should reflect your priorities and proclivities. For example, you might include time spent talking with your spouse, playing with your children or listening to music. You might enjoy reading novels, playing tennis or exercising. The point is that every minute you spend chasing current events is a minute you can't spend doing the things you love. Your list prevents you from overlooking that fact.

6. Ask your family to refrain from watching the news on television in your home. You might otherwise be tempted to sit down and watch it with them.

   It is important that you remove the object of your addiction from your environment. Consider that during drug rehabilitation, patients are told to sever ties with friends and acquaintances who continue to take illicit substances. Failing to do so would provide too great a temptation to surrender to their cravings. So it is with your addiction to current events.

Your family may not understand your desire to avoid watching the news. If that's the case, sit down and explain it to them. Then, ask for their help. For example, if they must watch the news at home, ask them to do so in their rooms rather than in the living room.

Day 25

Stop Focusing On The 80% That Doesn't Matter

The 80/20 rule, sometimes called the Pareto principle, states that 80% of your results will stem from 20% of your actions. The implication is that 80% of your actions will have little impact on your long-term goals. That means you're probably wasting a lot of time and effort working on tasks of questionable value.

The Pareto principle is so named for the man that came up with it. Vilfredo Pareto, an Italian economist, wrote a paper in the late 1800s claiming that 80% of the land in his country was owned by 20% of the people.

Today, the 80/20 rule is commonly discussed in the context of productivity. For example, time management experts often refer to it when they talk about task analysis and prioritization.

Most people attack their work with little regard for priority. Every task on their to-do lists is treated with equal importance. The problem, according to the 80/20 rule, is that most of the to-do items we spend time on are unimportant in relation to our goals. We can skip 80% of them without experiencing serious consequences.

For example, consider salespeople. Most of them will admit a majority percentage of their sales come from a small percentage of their customers. That's the 80/20 principle at work.

Consider work-related projects. In many cases, the majority of the workload is handled by a minority number of parties. Corporate managers know that 80% of the work in their departments is done by 20% of their staff.

Marketers know that 80% of their sales stem from 20% of their advertising campaigns. Customer service managers know that 80% of customer complaints come from 20% of their customers. CEOs know that 80% of their companies' revenues are generated by 20% of their products.

The 80/20 rule is simple. That's one of its charms. And it carries major implications for the manner in which you should prioritize your to-do lists. The problem is, the rule is often misunderstood and applied incorrectly.

For example, many people insist the 80% of tasks on their to-do lists that deliver little long-term value must still be completed. They claim such tasks can't simply be ignored.

While that may be true, it disregards a more salient point: tasks that deliver little value warrant less time and attention than tasks that deliver considerable value.

For example, suppose you need to respond to emails from coworkers, an activity you've determined provides negligible value to your goals. You can't just ignore the emails. But you *can* avoid spending a lot of time writing them. That's a proper application of the Pareto principle.

When we apply the rule correctly, we spend more time on tasks that matter and less on tasks that matter less. We not only get more things done, but we get the *right* things done.

When we apply the rule incorrectly, or neglect to apply it at all, we risk creating obstacles that impede our productivity.

How This Bad Habit Hurts Your Productivity

Neglecting to prioritize the tasks on your to-do list impacts your workflow in five ways. First, as noted above, you end up focusing on the wrong things. You spend too much time working on low-value items, and consequently lack sufficient time to complete high-value items.

Second, you become more inclined to mistake being busy for being productive. Working on a series of low-value tasks gives you the impression that you're getting a lot done. But the tasks you're working on merely keep you busy. Completing them doesn't move you significantly toward your goals.

Third, you end up spending your limited time on unimportant items that should be disregarded or delegated to others. Without a system of prioritization, you have no way to identify which tasks deserve your attention first, or at all. You thus have no choice but to address the entire lot, even the ones that are unlikely to move the needle on your results. Low-value tasks are assigned the same priority as high-value tasks, which severely dilutes your productivity.

Fourth, neglecting the 80/20 rule eventually leads to frustration, discouragement, disillusionment and burnout. You feel continuously busy thanks to a long, never-ending list of low-value tasks, but never make significant advancement toward your objectives. Burnout erodes your motivation to work. That, in turn, causes your productivity to plummet.

Fifth, because you're perpetually busy with low-value tasks, you enjoy fewer opportunities to rest. That increases your stress levels and reduces your ability to concentrate. Both side effects cripple your ability to work efficiently and meet deadlines with minimal errors.

Today's goal is to apply the 80/20 rule in every area of your life in which you hope to become more productive. That may include your job, home life, hobbies, relationships and building a side business. Following are four easy steps you can take to get maximum value from the Pareto principle.

Action Steps

1. Create a list of low-value, low-priority tasks. These are the items you can confidently ignore or delegate to others.

   For example, if you're a teacher, you might spend an inordinate amount of time filing students' papers in their respective cubby holes. If you have a classroom aid, ask her to file the papers for you.

   Suppose you're a small business owner and have spent dozens of hours creating and updating your company's website. Unless you're an astute designer, that's a poor use of your time. Hire a web designer and spend your limited time doing what you do best.

   The key is to create a list of tasks you can easily review. With that list in front of you, there will be little confusion about the items that deserve your time and attention.

2. Monitor how you spend your time. Keep a daily log for at least two weeks. At the end of that time frame, review it to identify areas that warrant your attention.

   Tracking how you use your time is crucial if you hope to increase your productivity. (We discussed this concept briefly in Days 8 and 19.) Here, the goal is to focus on the amount of time you normally devote to the tasks that appear on the list you created in Action Step #1.

3. Look for opportunities to use the 80/20 rule to streamline other areas of your life. For example, apply it to your exercise regimen; focus on the few exercises that deliver the most noticeable results. Apply it to your internet surfing; focus on the few sites that give

you the most enjoyment. Apply it to your household chores; focus your effort on the chores that deliver the biggest results.

Growing accustomed to using the Pareto principle is like developing any new habit. It is reinforced through repeated, consistent application. By applying it in various ways, you'll form a pattern of behavior that will have a positive effect on your overall ability to get things done.

4. Hire an assistant. There are many services online that will handle low-value or low-priority tasks for you. These services offer to do everything from respond to your emails and pay your monthly bills to research topics and shop for gifts for your loved ones. You can find these services by typing "hire virtual assistant" at Google.

Alternatively, hire a local high-school student. A few hours a week should suffice. Once you train this individual, you can trust him or her to handle simple to-do items with care and at low cost.

The point is to delegate low-value tasks that cannot be ignored nor eliminated. Doing so will allow you to devote more of your limited time to activities that truly deserve your attention and focus.

Day 26

Stop Getting Caught Up In Unnecessary Drama

❝ Drama is life with the dull bits cut out.❞
- Alfred Hitchcock

For some of us, conflict is a drug. We love to watch as drama engulfs those around us. Whether we're listening to gossip or watching our coworkers feud, strife among others has a near-hypnotic effect on us.

That's one of the reasons reality television is so popular. It caters to our inner voyeurs.

Our eagerness for drama stems from a variety of factors. Some people enjoy it because it gives them an outlet to passive-aggressively air their grievances. For example, suppose two people are arguing because one finds the other's behavior irritating. The drama enthusiast will use the opportunity to express his or her own irritation about the latter party's behavior.

Other people are drawn to conflict because they want to help resolve it. They suffer from "white knight syndrome," an irresistible need to rescue others. Doing so makes them feel important and valued among their peers.

Still others are attracted to drama for the entertainment it offers. They live vicariously through it. They feel their lives are unexciting, and see strife among their peers as a way to liven things up.

Yet others are drawn to it because they yearn for a distraction that will banish their boredom. They're unmotivated to work, and their apathy prompts them to look for diversions. When one surfaces, they immediately gravitate toward it.

A significant amount of time and energy are wasted every day on unnecessary and destructive feuds, both in the workplace and at home. In the workplace, it may arise in the form of office politics. At home, clashes might occur between family members.

The involved parties devote considerable time and attention to gossiping, defending themselves against others' allegations and making their adversaries appear to be culpable for any number of transgressions.

Worse, the turmoil has a ripple effect. As more people become involved in the conflict, sides are chosen, responses are crafted and outcomes are calculated.

Meanwhile, little work is getting done.

Clearly, getting embroiled in drama, both at work and at home, will only diminish your ability to get things done in a time-efficient manner.

How This Bad Habit Hurts Your Productivity

The more you get caught up in drama, the more often you'll deal with interruptions. Listening - or worse, participating - in gossip, consoling victims or joining antagonists sends a message that you're available.

You're the only person you can count on to protect your time. If you fail to do so, others will interrupt you. Their interruptions will play havoc with your momentum and productivity.

Another consequence of getting involved in others' conflicts is that you become more susceptible to distractions. The drama promises more excitement than the tasks on your to-do list. As such, you become more and more inclined to drop whatever you're doing to spectate.

In the 2009 animated film "Up" (by Pixar), a dog named Dug was constantly distracted by squirrels. Their presence would distract him to the point that he would stop mid-sentence - he was able to communicate through a special collar - and whip his head around to look for them.

Many people react the same way to even the slightest hint of conflict among their peers. In doing so, they forfeit their momentum and waste precious time.

Becoming entangled in drama also tarnishes your image. Your peers - coworkers, friends and family members - see you choosing sides. If you choose the "wrong" side (or at least wrong in their opinion), you jeopardize your reputation.

That may seem unfair. Nonetheless, the risk is real.

Getting caught up in others' disputes also generates needless friction between you and your coworkers. Your participation, even as an observer, can be perceived as lending support to one side or the other. Tempers can easily flare, causing the hostility between the quarreling parties to escalate.

As the respective camps "circle their wagons," it becomes more and more difficult to work together. That can have a profound effect on your productivity if you rely on others for data or other deliverables during the course of your day.

Another side effect of involving yourself in others' drama is stress. You become less productive, more distracted and more vulnerable to constant interruptions while your to-do list grows unchecked. You're left with less time and focus to get things done, which places increased pressure on you. Meanwhile, the friction that arises between you and your coworkers creates unnecessary obstacles that impede your ability to complete projects.

If you find that you're regularly mired in others' feuds, it's time to make a change. Below, you'll find seven action steps that will help you to break this destructive habit and return your focus to your work.

Action Steps

1. Familiarize yourself with the types of personalities that create drama. Once you're aware of them, you can take steps to lessen your exposure to them.

   For example, some people are adept at portraying themselves as victims. They rarely admit fault when given feedback, and instead point to others' rudeness or general unfairness. Other people seem drawn to the role of harasser. They not only regularly find fault in their peers, but often give voice to their misgivings. Still others gravitate to the role of rescuer. These individuals take it upon themselves to defend perceived victims wherever conflicts arise.

2. Limit your exposure to the victims, harassers and rescuers in your work environment. Doing so will help to insulate you from useless, time-wasting drama.

   Also, reevaluate any relationships that expose you to unnecessary negativity. For example, steer clear of people who constantly complain about unpleasant circumstances. Keep your distance from individuals who regularly try to enlist you to their sides in arguments with their peers. Rebuff those who tend to be manipulative, plotting against and sabotaging others' efforts for their own gain.

3. Shun all gossip. Nothing good springs from talking about another person behind his or her back. On the contrary, the

144

practice encourages the establishment of cliques. That, in turn, erects unnecessary walls between parties, which causes workplace productivity to deteriorate.

If the gossip is about you, don't bother defending yourself. There lies a rabbit hole that can engulf your time and attention to the detriment of your work. Remind yourself that gossip is comprised of rumors, vague insinuations, spiteful commentary and wild speculation. If someone asks you a question, respond with the facts. Then, get back to work. By doing so consistently, you'll be perceived as a trustworthy source of information who has little interest in nonsense. Accordingly, gossip about you will quickly lose its allure and influence.

4. When someone attempts to share gossip with you, ask that person to explain his or her reasons for doing so. That should stop the gossiper in his or her tracks.

   People gossip to feel superior over others. But few are willing to admit it. When they're asked to explain themselves, most stammer and desist. That's to your benefit since your goal is to avoid gossip.

5. Allow victims to fend for themselves. You'll earn a reputation for rebuffing those who constantly blame others for their troubles and try to enlist others to their defense.

   Few victims exhaust their options before seeking help from potential rescuers. If a coworker approaches you and voices displeasure over a perceived slight by another person, immediately stop him or her. Ask whether he or she has discussed the slight with the person in question. If not, require that such a conversation take place before seeking your involvement.

6. If a victim attempts to recruit you to his or her side, empathize and explain that you're busy. Most victims, when pressed, will refrain from claiming their circumstances deserve a higher priority than your work. Instead, they'll look elsewhere for a potential rescuer.

   This is an alternative approach than the one recommended in Action Step #5. In that step, there was a possibility of getting involved after the victim talks to the harasser. Here, you're making it clear that you intend to abstain from the conflict altogether.

7. Be clear in everything you say to others. Clear communication makes it difficult for people to misconstrue your words, intentionally or otherwise.

   That makes you a poor target for gossip. It will also help you to build a reputation as an honest and forthright person who has little patience for drama.

Day 27

Stop Working Without Concrete Goals

❝❝ The game has its ups and downs, but you can never lose focus of your individual goals and you can't let yourself be beat because of lack of effort." - Michael Jordan

Our goals give us direction. They give us something to shoot for. They also show us the culmination of our efforts. For example, if you're for a promotion at your job, being awarded that promotion is evidence your efforts were worthwhile.

Goals also make us accountable. If we fail to achieve them, we're given an opportunity to acknowledge our failures and look for areas in our workflow that warrant improvement. Our goals give us a gauge by which to measure our progress, and the impetus to make adjustments as needed.

That's empowering. Working toward concrete objectives provides ongoing feedback. In the event we fail to achieve them, the feedback prompts us to look for problems or to reevaluate our expectations (or both).

Surprisingly, many people work without goals. They have no vision regarding where they want to be at any given point in their lives. Or, if they have such a vision, it's little more than a fantasy. They lack a strategy for making it a reality. Instead, they live day to day, hoping for good fortune, and never truly feel in control of their fate.

There's even a movement that caters to that attitude. It proposes to work without goals, claiming that setting them does nothing for one's productivity or success. Proponents argue that setting goals is useless since doing so suggests an individual has control over events that are, in reality, beyond his or her influence.

I disagree with that fatalistic line of reasoning. Moreover, I suspect many people rely on it as a way to rationalize their lax attitudes toward goal-setting. They neglect to set them out of laziness, and excuse their inaction with the delusion that setting them is a waste of time.

As you'll see in the following section, working without clear purpose impairs your ability to work efficiently and manage your time effectively.

How This Bad Habit Hurts Your Productivity

Neglecting to establish well-defined goals negatively impacts your productivity in seven ways. First, it robs you of direction. I mentioned above that our goals serve as a gauge of our progress. Without them, we have no reliable way to know whether we're on the right course. As philosopher Thomas Carlyle once said, "A man without a goal is like a ship without a rudder."

Second, it wears down your motivation to optimize your workflow. Without explicit objectives, there's no sense of urgency. Without urgency, there's little inducement to seek improvements in our productivity.

Third, a lack of clear-cut goals lessens your focus on end results. Without that focus, you're more likely to be distracted. That, in turn, leads to forfeited momentum and wasted time.

Fourth, you're prevented from benefiting from the valuable feedback loop made possible by goals.

Suppose your efforts fail to effect a specific outcome. You need a mechanism that informs you of that failure. Only then will you be made aware of potential problems in your workflow. And only then are you likely to seek a solution to those problems. Failure isn't necessarily bad. It's merely feedback regarding your current approach. It tells you that something you're doing isn't generating the desired results. Without goals, you miss the advantage of that feedback loop.

A fifth consequence of working without goals is that you never feel as if you're making any real progress. Despite working hard and devoting considerable time, you never get the impression that your efforts are moving things forward. There's no accurate gauge by which to evaluate the results of your labor.

Sixth, without goals, you lack the ability to create a roadmap toward high-priority outcomes.

For example, suppose you're 40 years old and would like to retire early. Retirement at any age under 65 requires that you have a significant amount of money saved, ideally in safe, income-generating investments. Suppose, however, you don't know the precise age at which you hope to retire (i.e. you have no clear objective). That being the case, there's no way for you to develop a reliable plan for amassing the needed savings. Instead, you're left to sock away money haphazardly and hope for the best.

Can you imagine how that "strategy" might result in your disappointment?

The more explicit your goals, the more refined your plans for achieving them. The more refined your plans, the greater the likelihood you'll accomplish what you set out to do.

So it is with having goals related to your productivity.

Lastly, without goals, you have no reliable way to measure your effectiveness. After all, as mentioned above, you don't have the advantage of a feedback loop. Consequently, you have no way to know whether you're truly competent and skilled in your work, or need to improve in one or more areas.

The result? You'll suffer a decline in self-confidence. That increases your aversion to risk, which makes you less likely to try new things.

If you've been neglecting to establish firm, explicit goals related to your workflow, now's the time to start. Use the following five action steps to make doing so a habit.

Action Steps

1. Brainstorm where you'd like to end up concerning every area of your life. Think about your long-term objectives related to your career, family life, financial position and physical health. Consider your mental well-being, attitude toward life and general happiness.

   For example, suppose you work in your employer's marketing department. You hope to one day be named your company's Director of Marketing.

   Or suppose you're 40 years old and have $250,000 in savings and investments. You aim to amass $1 million by the time you retire.

   Do this exercise with the end in mind. You'll find it's a fun activity that will clarify what you hope to achieve in every aspect of your life.

2. Break down your long-term objectives into small, bite-sized goals.

The goals we defined in Action Step #1 are lifelong. That being the case, they're difficult to contemplate in the context of your daily routine. For example, you might know that you need to save $750,000 before you retire, but what specific actions should you take *today* to move closer toward that goal?

By breaking down your long-term aspirations into short-term aims, you'll be able to more easily formulate a plan for achieving them. You'll know what you need to do on a daily, weekly or monthly basis.

For example, if you aspire to become your company's marketing director, you'll need to turn in good work on time and regularly do so in a way that exceeds your boss's expectations. You may also need to present innovative, workable solutions to the marketing problems your company faces.

Once you break down your lifetime goals into daily and weekly tasks, you can add those tasks to your to-do lists. Your goals thus become *actionable*.

3. Create each small goal using the S.M.A.R.T. system. A "SMART" goal is one that is specific, measurable, attainable, relevant and time-sensitive. Assigning those characteristics to an objective gives it more weight and relevance.

By way of illustration, let's return to our long-term goal of saving $750,000 before you retire at age 65. Assuming you're 40 years old, you'll need to save $30,000 a year for 25 years, or $2,500 a month. (For simplicity, I'm ignoring the capital appreciation of your current investments.)

That goal is *specific*.

It's also *measurable*. If you only manage to save $2,000 next month, you'll know immediately that you're behind schedule.

Whether saving $2,500 a month is *attainable* depends on your income level.

Your goal is *relevant* because it is focused on allowing you to retire with a specific amount of money in the bank ($750,000).

Lastly, it's *time-sensitive*. You have a monthly deadline. You know when the deadline expires each month.

This is a far different approach to goal-setting than the one followed by most people. Most people have dreams. They have aspirations with no clear-cut plans to achieve them.

4. Prioritize each small goal. Do so in the context of how important your long-term aspirations are to you.

For example, suppose that in addition to becoming the marketing director for your company, you also want to become a proficient yachtsman. The first goal may require you to work on weekends (climbing the corporate ladder can be brutal). Unfortunately, weekends may be the only opportunity you have to improve your nautical skills.

It is only by prioritizing your short-term goals according to the importance you place on your long-term aspirations that you can choose which tasks to focus on.

5. Pay attention to your performance, not whether a specific short-term goal is achieved.

This Action Step might seem to contradict the ideas we've discussed thus far. But it's important to focus on things you can control.

Let's return to our example of wanting to become your company's Director of Marketing. As we noted, that long-term goal entails turning in good work on time and consistently exceeding your boss's expectations. You control the quality and timeliness with which you deliver your projects. But you have little control over whether your boss likes you enough to promote you.

Definitely establish objectives that steer your daily workflow. But don't get too engrossed over whether you're able to achieve them when they're influenced by factors beyond your control. Instead, focus on your personal performance.

Day 28

Stop Letting Your Phone Run Your Life

Our phones improve our lives in countless ways. We're more accessible than ever to the people who are important to us. We can obtain information whenever we need it. We can easily record important events using our phones' cameras. And handy tools, such as calculators, flashlights, recipes and GPS apps are always at our fingertips.

But as useful as our phones are to us, they can be just as much a foe as friend. Many people are addicted to their phones, unable to go more than a few minutes without checking them. Pew Research published an exhaustive study in 2015 in which 46% of participants noted they "couldn't live without their phones."

That dependency carries consequences. From watching videos and checking social media to listening to music and texting friends, our phones dictate whether or not we use our time productively.

Smartphone addiction is more prevalent than you might imagine, and it doesn't discriminate by age or gender. A 4th-grade girl is just as likely to exhibit signs of addiction as the male CEO of a Fortune 500 company.

How do you know if you're addicted? Here are some common signs...

- Do you often hope, while driving, to hit red traffic lights so you can safely check and send texts?

- Do you instinctively grab your phone when you feel awkward?
- Do you find yourself incessantly checking your texts, emails and social media accounts, cycling through them multiple times?
- Is your phone a constant presence when you and your significant other go out for dinner?
- Do you check your phone while eating meals, watching television and spending time with your family?

If you answered yes to any of the above questions, you're probably addicted to your phone. As you'll see below, your addiction can interfere with your daily productivity.

How This Bad Habit Hurts Your Productivity

Like any type of addiction, this one reinforces itself with each application. Every time you reach for your phone in any given circumstance, you train yourself to do so when that circumstance recurs.

You know from experience that your phone can hamper your productivity. But you may not have considered the many ways in which it does so.

First, it destroys your momentum. You might tell yourself that you'll only check for new texts, but once you have your phone in hand, it's too hard to resist checking email. You might even be tempted to check your voicemails and Facebook updates.

Recall from earlier chapters that each break in your momentum sets you back at least 20 minutes. That's how long it takes to get back on track.

Second, your phone addiction diminishes your creativity. If

you're like most people, you need time without a flood of visual stimuli to allow your creative juices to flow. Incessantly checking your phone creates a continuous loop of stimuli. Your mind is never given an opportunity to drift or rest.

Third, your phone makes you more prone to distractions. Reaching for it every 10 minutes is like a sugar addict reaching for a cookie or piece of cake. Every time you do it, you reinforce the habit. The stronger the habit becomes, the weaker your defenses against distractions.

Fourth, your phone makes you less present during meetings and conversations. When you check social media, send emails or reply to texts, you're unable to pay attention to the people around you. (Moreover, you're probably not as good at faking it as you might think.)

Fifth, being obsessed with your phone makes you more likely to play games and use time-wasting apps. That, in turn, will slow down your workflow and hurt your ability to get things done.

To be sure, it's important to take breaks and enjoy various forms of entertainment. Your brain needs to disconnect periodically to stay fresh. The problem with your phone is that it's a constant temptation, threatening to lure you away from your work at inopportune times.

Sixth, your phone addiction will make you more inclined to confuse busyness with efficiency. With your phone always in hand, it's easy to fall into the trap of thinking you're getting a lot done. In reality, your phone is filling your day with unnecessary tasks, such as checking Facebook, posting "tweets" on Twitter and responding to friends' texts.

It's time to get your phone habit under control. Following are six action steps designed to help you do that.

Action Steps

1. Turn off your phone during time blocks you've scheduled to work on high-value tasks. You presumably set aside the time because the tasks are important to you. Don't let your phone ruin your momentum and focus with its chirps, rings and other alerts.

   At first, this step will be difficult. That's understandable. You're working against years of self-imposed conditioning. But repeated application over time will make it easier. Plus, you'll begin to notice your productivity rising during these time blocks.

2. Refrain from checking your phone out of boredom. Boredom is one of the most common reasons we reach for our phones.

   You can see evidence of this if you visit your local Starbucks. Pay attention to the folks waiting for drinks. More than half of them will be on their phones, checking Facebook, reading texts or "Googling" information that has little value to them.

   Don't use your phone as a crutch for boredom. Learn to live without it. The less often you reach for it, the more engaged you'll be with your surroundings, your work and the people near you.

3. Define the times and places you'll allow yourself to check your phone. For example, you might permit yourself to do so while eating breakfast at home and while eating lunch at the office. You might also designate the period between 6:00 p.m. and 7:00 p.m. to be "phone time."

   The point of doing this step is to preclude yourself from using your phone outside your designated times and places. For example, you'll be less likely to grab your phone while enjoying dinner with your family.

4. Define the activities you'll use your phone to perform. Limit the list to five items.

For example, commit to using your phone for responding to emails and texts, making important phone calls and looking for driving directions. Refrain from using it for other purposes, such as engaging followers on Twitter and posting photos on Instagram.

The point is, when you act with intention, you'll be less likely to waste time. Shunning social media (on the phone) is just an example. I do it because the activity can so easily become a time sink.

5. Monitor your phone usage throughout the day. Track how many times you check it and how much time you spend on it each session. Do this for two weeks. That should be enough time for trends to emerge.

As we've discussed in previous chapters, tracking how you use your time is a critical part of increasing your productivity. You may be surprised by how much time slips through your fingers each day thanks to your phone.

6. Turn your phone off when you go to bed. Otherwise, the alerts and notifications may disturb your sleep.

Also, if you take your phone to bed, you'll be tempted to check social media, play games and respond to emails and texts. These things can easily draw you in and siphon away time that can be better used to get a good night's sleep.

Put your phone somewhere out of reach from your bed. That way, you won't be tempted to grab it to take "one last look at Facebook." Instead, use the time to enjoy seven or eight hours of restful slumber. You'll be more productive and better able to retain information the following day.

Day 29

Stop Working Until You Burn Out

Have you ever felt emotionally and physically drained to the point that you stop caring? If so, you've likely experienced burnout.

At its simplest, it's the result of accumulated stress. You feel as if you're buried under your responsibilities with too few resources to dig yourself out. You feel overwhelmed.

With time, you become discouraged by your circumstances and begin to view the foreseeable future as bleak and hopeless. Your enthusiasm for your work deteriorates and you eventually find reasons to avoid it altogether.

The result? Your productivity plummets to the point that finishing tasks, even simple ones, becomes a monumental chore. Meeting deadlines becomes a fool's errand.

The causes of burnout vary from person to person, and differ according to environment. For example, many people burn out because they feel have little control over their workflow and output. Their entire day is spent responding to the needs and whims of others.

Other folks feel drained due to their workload. They have too much to do and not enough time to do it.

Still others burn out due to insufficient sleep, an unhealthy diet, over-responsiveness to others' needs and a lack of supportive friends.

The point is that burnout is real, can occur for a variety of reasons and will have a significant impact on your ability to get things done.

Hence, it pays to take steps to prevent it. That entails being able to recognize the telltale signs:

- Do you feel unmotivated to take action of any kind?
- Is the quality of your work slipping?
- Are you indifferent to your poor-quality output?
- Do you find yourself becoming irritable with others?
- Are you having difficulty sleeping?
- Is your outlook overly-cynical?
- Do you often feel tired, even after a good night's rest?
- Have you lost your appetite?
- Do you no longer find joy in spending time with your family?

These symptoms indicate you're working too hard and consequently, feeling both mentally and physically fatigued. They signal that your current circumstances are unsustainable. Something must change in order for you to get back on track and regain your lost enthusiasm.

In the event you lack the motivation to make the necessary changes, it's worth reviewing how burnout affects your productivity.

How This Bad Habit Hurts Your Productivity

Burnout interferes with your ability to get things done in five notable ways.

First, it induces a feeling of helplessness. You become convinced that you lack the necessary influence or resources to change your circumstances. That, in turn, consigns you to perpetuating the cycle of stress that led to your burnout in the first place.

Second, it makes you more inclined to be resentful toward others.

You begin to feel as if your bosses, coworkers, friends or family members are taking advantage of you. Resentment saps your energy, which prevents you from focusing on your work.

Third, burnout sets the stage for exhaustion. Emotional fatigue gives rise to physical fatigue. Before long, you may reach the point at which you're unmotivated to get out of bed in the morning much less do your best work.

Fourth, it fills you with an enduring sense of failure as you continue to miss deadlines, make mistakes and produce low-quality work. In that way, burnout becomes a self-perpetuating cycle of stress. Stress drains your energy and taxes your emotional health. That causes your work-related performance to slip. Your slipping performance leads to feedback from your boss and coworkers, which prompts additional stress.

Fifth, the more stress, resentment and lack of motivation you experience, the further your productivity will decline. So much of your energy will be spent coping with negative emotions that little will be left to help you get things done.

The good news is that there's a solution for burnout. The following steps will help you to prevent it, or recover from it if you're currently caught in its grasp.

Action Steps

1. Perform a monthly self-evaluation. Look for common signs of burnout (see above).

    There are many ways to approach this type of self-analysis. The method I've found to be most helpful is to create a list of questions, each of which asks whether I'm experiencing a particular symptom of burnout.

For example, I ask myself "Am I regularly frustrated with my daily workflow?" and "Do I feel overwhelmed with too many tasks?" I'll then score each question from 1 to 10 to reflect my current perspective and attitude. A "10" indicates I'm nearing my breaking point.

Come up with a set of questions that highlights the personal circumstances you face on the path to burnout. Answer them once a month.

2. Schedule breaks throughout the day. Treat them like mini-appointments with yourself. Don't miss them.

This step is often overlooked or dismissed because of its simplicity. It's almost pedestrian. But taking breaks can mean the difference between maintaining a high level of productivity throughout the day and teetering on the verge of burnout.

3. Commit to ending the day at a specific time - for example, 6:00 p.m. If your boss asks you to stay late, resist and explain your reasoning (you need to rest so you can perform at your best level tomorrow).

Too often, we're tempted to put in extra hours to get more work done. The problem is, doing so on a regular basis takes a toll on our mental and physical resources. Moreover, it's a sign that you're either overloaded with responsibilities or not working productively during normal work hours.

4. Take weekends off. Set aside unfinished tasks for Monday.

Don't allow work to encroach on time that is better spent relaxing and recovering from the previous workweek. Doing so may make you feel as if you're getting more things done in the short run, but increases your susceptibility to burnout in the long run.

To be fair, there may be times during which working on the weekends is unavoidable. But those times should be the exceptions that define the rule.

5. Limit the amount of time you spend on your phone.

As we noted yesterday (see Day 28), your phone can be a constant source of distraction. Few people can resist the temptation to check their texts and email when they hear the pings alerting them of new messages. And once they check their messages, it's easy to rationalize checking Facebook, Twitter and Instagram.

The problem here is twofold. First, the continuous stimuli prevents your brain from taking a break. Second, you're always connected to others. You're always "on call," even if that's not your intention. If you routinely respond to texts and emails as soon as you receive them, people will expect you to do so whenever they reach out to you.

Put your phone away during times you don't need it.

6. Periodically review your responsibilities and evaluate how they align with your short and long-term goals. You may find they no longer do so.

Take the opportunity to free up extra time and reduce the amount of energy you put into low-value tasks. Purge any and all that have no bearing on your goals. Assign a lower priority to tasks that contribute to your goals, but do so in a negligible fashion.

7. Stop multitasking. We talked about the practice in Day 16, but it's worth mentioning again in the context of avoiding burnout.

When you multitask, you force your brain to switch back and forth between concurrent activities. That increases the amount of pressure you put on your mental faculties. You becomes less able to concentrate, less able to filter extraneous information and less able to commit new data to memory. With time, the added pressure to maintain your job performance increases your stress levels.

Work on one thing at a time. There are few emergencies that warrant dividing your attention.

8. Start each day with a morning ritual designed to motivate and inspire you. Your ritual will set the tone for the rest of the day.

Many people drag themselves out of bed, dump coffee down their gullets and jump into their vehicles to fight traffic on the way to work. That's a depressing way to start the day.

You can do better.

Think about the activities you enjoy doing when you have free time. They might include practicing yoga, going for a brisk walk or writing in a journal.

Wake up 15 minutes earlier each morning and spend that extra time doing one of those activities. You'll find that it puts you in a calm frame of mind that's less vulnerable to stress.

Day 30
Stop Allowing Stress Into Your Life

" If you ask what is the single most important key to longevity, I would have to say it is avoiding worry, stress and tension." - George Burns

Yesterday, we talked about burnout. One of the main contributors to burnout is stress. Today, we're going to take a closer look at stress in the context of how it affects your productivity even in the absence of burnout.

First, it's important to understand the nature of stress. What emotions does it trigger? What are its most common sources? And of course, what steps should you take to prevent it from negatively impacting your ability to work?

Stress is highly subjective. One person's anxiety is another person's calm. But at its core, it defines the body's response to a perceived threat. If you had lived in prehistoric times, you would have experienced it had you stumbled upon a sabertooth tiger. Today, we deal with an entirely different set of circumstances that trigger our body's stress response.

Stress may surface as a result of our workload, pressure from our bosses or arguments with our spouses. It can rear its head due to financial problems, health issues or even loud noise in our immediate environment. Our stress levels also increase in the wake of traumatic experiences, such as getting a divorce or caring for a terminally-ill loved one.

Periodic stress is unavoidable. It's a part of life. The key is to find ways to allow it to dissipate. When it persists, it can have a disastrous effect on your mental and physical well-being. That effect carries a steep invoice with regard to your productivity.

Stress can affect your emotional health. It can make you feel irritable, lonely and overwhelmed.

It can affect your physical health. Long periods of increased tension and anxiety can impair your digestion, reduce your libido and cause chest pain.

It can wreak havoc with your brain. Longstanding stress can hobble your ability to focus, erode your memory and fill you with a sense of despair and helplessness.

Uninterrupted stress also makes us more likely to procrastinate, eat poorly and get too little sleep.

The negative impact of stress on our lives is unmistakable. Fortunately, we're not without tools for dealing with it. We can deflect it. We can shun it. We can give it a wide berth, preventing it from affecting our lives.

The problem is, most people are unaware they possess the tools to do so. Their lack of awareness allows their stress levels to build until they eventually cause adverse effects.

Worse, many people are unaware they're dealing with high levels of persistent stress. Maybe they've lived with it their entire lives and grown accustomed to it. They don't realize there's a better way to live. Or maybe their stress levels have risen so gradually that they don't realize it's having a dramatic effect on their ability to get things done.

How This Bad Habit Hurts Your Productivity

We touched briefly on the negative effects of stress in previous chapters. We'll revisit some of them below along with a few that have, to this point, gone unmentioned.

First, long-term stress can lead to mental and physical fatigue. After enduring weeks of continuous tension, you'll feel tired and worn out despite getting eight hours of sleep each night. This is a sign you're on the precipice of burnout.

Second, consider the impacts to your health. Ongoing stress can cause headaches, breathing difficulties and tachycardia (rapid heart rate). It can cause nausea, back pain and diarrhea. If you have arthritis, stress can worsen it. If you have asthma, stress can aggravate it. These and other physiological side effects will diminish your ability to work productively.

Third, studies show that long-term stress can impair your ability to process and store new information. That, in turn, will inhibit your concentration and recall.

Fourth, you'll make more mistakes. Diminished focus translates into a higher error rate. Time spent correcting those errors will cause your productivity to crumble.

Fifth, because high stress levels hamper your focus, cause you to feel fatigued and increase your error rate, you'll spend more time completing tasks. That can affect your ability to turn in projects on time.

Sixth, stress can make you short-tempered. Your irritability can damage the relationships you share with your coworkers, friends and family members.

Again, stress is a part of life. But that doesn't mean you're a helpless victim. On the contrary, you can take simple steps to minimize its long-term impact on your workflow and productivity.

Action Steps

1. Identify the triggers that are causing you to feel stress. The easiest way to do so is to keep a journal. When you start to notice signs of tension, write down the triggers. What is happening in your environment that is making you feel tense?

Maintain your "stress journal" for at least two weeks. That will allow trends to surface.

2. Develop healthy ways to respond to elevated stress levels. Some people respond to stress in ways that further impedes their productivity. For example, they eat junk food, drink alcohol or refuse to get out of bed.

If you do similarly unhealthy things in response to tension, come up with a list of healthy alternatives. For example, commit to taking a 15-minute walk outside rather than grabbing the closest sugary snack.

3. Work fewer hours. In Day 7, we talked about the merits of refusing to work overtime. In Day 29, we talked about the merits of keeping your weekends work-free. This step is an extension of that recommendation.

If you're experiencing a high level of workplace stress, try to set boundaries that prevent you from working long hours. For example, if you routinely find yourself working until 8:00 p.m., commit to setting your work aside at 6:00 p.m. With solid time management skills, you'll end up getting the same amount of work done. Meanwhile you'll have more time to relax, which will lower your stress levels.

4. Review why you love your work. Sometimes, longstanding stress stemming from our daily experience so completely hobbles our enthusiasm that we forget the reasons we enjoy our work. Take 10 minutes to remind yourself of those reasons. What aspects of your work give you a sense of satisfaction and fulfillment?

If you dislike your work, it may be time to look for other opportunities.

5. Limit the number of tasks on your to-do lists. We discussed this idea at length in Day 3. The most important thing to remember is to cap the number of items at five. Any more would risk making you feel overwhelmed and unnecessarily stressed.

6. Delegate tasks. We talked about delegation in Day 8. You don't need to do everything yourself. In fact, you shouldn't even try.

   Identify reliable individuals and assign them tasks according to their respective skill sets. Then, give them the space they need to complete those tasks.

   There is an art and science to proper delegation. Both extend beyond the scope of this action guide. It's enough to highlight its value as a means to manage your stress levels.

7. Put an end to unnecessary interruptions. Doing so will allow you to concentrate on the task in front of you, giving you an opportunity to build the momentum that comes with focused, undisturbed work.

   I've mentioned in previous chapters (see Days 12, 19, 21, 24 and 28) that a single disruption will set you back 20 minutes or more. Imagine being interrupted each hour by someone who "just needs a moment of your time." You would never get any real work done.

   Make it clear to your coworkers, friends and family members that you are not to be disturbed during time blocks you've scheduled for focused work. Eliminate needless interruptions and your stress level will plummet.

8. Reevaluate your relationships and purge those that are negative. For example, habitual complainers can take a major toll on your enthusiasm and motivation to get things done. Hanging around

them for extended periods can make you lethargic and apathetic. Either sever ties with such individuals or limit the amount of time you spend with them.

Instead, spend more time with those who are supportive. You'll find their enthusiasm is contagious and inspiring.

9. Start an exercise routine. In Day 22, we discussed how working out can improve your productivity. One of the ways it does so is by reducing your stress levels. Exercise releases endorphins, which are a natural stress reliever.

As I mentioned in Day 22, you don't have to commit hours to a daily workout regimen. Instead, take two or three 15-minute walks per day. You may be surprised by how calm and composed you feel after a brisk walk.

10. Remind yourself: "one thing at a time." You can only devote your attention to a single task at any one time. That's how the brain works (see Day 16 for more information). That being the case, there's no value in worrying about the tasks you're unable to address at any given moment.

So put them out of your mind.

For example, suppose you have to return three calls, finish a crucial report for your boss and review contractors' bids for an upcoming project. Don't allow stress to get the upper hand. Remind yourself "one thing at a time." Return each call, one by one, and don't worry about your boss's report or the contractors' bids. After you've made the calls, move onto the report. Finally, address the bids.

Worry about one task at a time. That will prevent you from feeling overwhelmed.

Bonus Material

10 Quick Tips For Taking Action
On The 30-Day Productivity Plan

First, congratulations on your commitment! The fact that you've completed this action guide is testament to your dedication to making positive changes in your life.

Second, the hard part is about to begin.

It does no good to claim otherwise. Breaking bad habits and forming new ones to take their place is difficult work. It involves identifying the triggers that prompt you to behave in certain ways and reconditioning your brain to respond differently to them.

That's the purpose of this bonus chapter.

Below, we're going to cover 10 quick tips for putting to use the Action Steps you've read over the last 30 days. Some of the following may be intuitive to you. Other tips might surprise you. All of them are important if you hope to become more productive in the weeks and months to come.

Let's get started…

Tip #1: Create a detailed plan for each habit.

Many people advise jumping in feet first when forming a new habit. They argue there's no reason to wait if you're serious about making a change.

But that's untrue. Diving in without a plan often does more harm than good.

Before dedicating yourself to breaking and replacing each bad habit described in this action guide, spend a day or two formulating a strategy. First, note your triggers - those circumstances that prompt the behavior you're trying to change. Second, make a list of people you can look to for support and feedback concerning your progress. Third, think about your personal stumbling blocks, and consider how you'll deal with them when they arise.

Tip #2: Be consistent.

Consistency is the key ingredient to success whenever you try to break a habit or develop a new one. Repeated application of the same behavior reinforces that behavior in your mind. It becomes an automatic response to certain triggers.

For example, you (hopefully) brush your teeth before going to bed each night. That activity has become ingrained in your mind after years of nightly application. It's automatic. In fact, you probably wouldn't feel right if you went to bed without brushing your teeth.

The habit is so strongly ingrained because of your consistency. Be likewise consistent when breaking the bad habits in this action guide and forming new ones to take their place.

Tip #3: Concentrate on building one habit at a time.

As noted above, breaking bad habits and forming new ones in their stead is difficult. It takes time, patience, self-discipline and grit. Relapse is common, especially with routines that are deeply-ingrained after years of repeated application.

For that reason, you should only try to change one habit at a time. That's tough enough. Changing several at once is a recipe for failure.

This action guide is organized as a 30-day plan. But that's merely to introduce each concept to you. The 30-day framework is to help you to understand how each bad habit impacts your productivity, and present the action steps you need to take in order to make a change. With that foundation in place, you can go about the task of actually breaking each habit and forming a new routine in its place.

Tackle one at a time. Be willing to spend a few weeks developing each new routine and making it a deeply-rooted pattern in your life.

Tip #4: Take small steps.

The most effective way to develop a new habit is to start small and make incremental progress toward your desired outcome. Taking huge leaps is likely to derail your efforts.

For example, consider exercise. We talked about it in Day 22. If you've been a couch potato for the last 10 years, it's unwise to start a new exercise regimen with a 5-mile run. Your body isn't ready for that level of physical exertion. You need to work up to that level.

A better approach is to start with a week of brisk walks. Then, start jogging during the second week. Add short runs - perhaps 3 to 5 minutes - during the third week.

Take small steps. There's no rush. Give yourself time to acclimate to each new routine. If you're consistent and diligent, you'll eventually effect your desired outcome.

Tip #5: Create a trigger for each new habit.

Triggers are an essential part of habit development. They serve as prompts for our behaviors. To that end, they make forming a new habit easier.

For example, suppose you're trying to write a novel. But you're having difficulty putting your backside into a chair and devoting time to getting it done. You need to create a trigger for the activity.

One idea is to enjoy a cup of coffee and afterward, immediately sit down and start writing. Follow that routine every day. Have a cup of coffee, and then start writing. Cup of coffee. Start writing. Coffee. Writing.

After a few weeks of consistent application, you'll find that drinking a cup of coffee will prompt you to work on your novel. It becomes your trigger.

Use this technique when forming new behaviors to replace the bad habits described throughout this book.

Tip #6: Write down each day's habit.

Writing a note helps to commit it to memory. There's something about the act of putting pen to paper that triggers are brains.

In 2014, the journal Psychological Science published a study showing that students taking notes using longhand were more likely to retain the information presented to them than students taking notes on their laptops.

Use that cognitive quirk to your advantage. Each morning, write down the habit you intend to focus on that day. You'll find that doing so will help you to remember it.

Tip #7: Involve others.

If you're like me, you tend to think you can do everything yourself. You don't need help from others.

But that's an illusion. In truth, we need others' support,

particularly when it comes to habit development. Don't be afraid to ask for help.

For example, recall Day 8 where we discussed the reasons to stop being a control freak. The idea was to curb the tendency of taking everything on yourself. To do that, you needed to get better at letting go of tasks and delegating them to others.

Suppose that's the habit you're trying to develop and reinforce. You need to know when you fail in that regard. You need feedback. To that end, ask your coworkers to tell you when you're assuming too many responsibilities at your office. Ask your family to do the same for you at home.

Enlist an accountability partner to whom you'll report your daily progress (or lack thereof).

Tip #8: Reward yourself for success.

Rewards are positive reinforcement. They serve as affirming feedback for good, healthy behaviors. That being the case, we should use them to help us form new habits.

Consider: we use dog treats with our canine friends to encourage certain behaviors (e.g. to come when we call). Our dogs learn to associate a desired outcome (something that tastes good) with specific routines. With consistent application, that causative association becomes so deeply-rooted in our pets that their behaviors become automatic.

Use that same approach on yourself. Reward yourself whenever you reach a defined benchmark (for example, focus for 40 minutes without getting distracted or running for 10 minutes without rest). The reward will motivate you to do it again, thereby reinforcing the habit.

Tip #9: Evaluate each failure.

It's tempting to disregard failures. After all, admitting defeat is unpleasant. It's much easier to sweep our flops under the rug where they'll be hidden from sight.

But there's value in reviewing our failures. They provide feedback on our processes and circumstances. They offer insight into changes we can make to streamline our efforts in developing new routines.

For example, in Day 9 we discussed the ways in which an unhealthy diet impacts your productivity. Suppose you commit to making a positive change by staying away from junk food. But rather than purging your kitchen of cookies, chips and ice cream, you store them away with the intention of simply not eating them.

Failure is almost guaranteed. You will relapse. The temptation is too great to resist. (I speak from experience.)

The key is that by evaluating your failure, you'll discover that keeping junk food in your home makes you far more likely to indulge yourself. You then know what you need to do in order to effect a better outcome.

When you fail, don't ignore it. Review the reasons. Try to identify the triggers for unhealthy or unproductive routines. Then, remove them.

Tip #10: Give yourself a break.

Breaking bad habits and replacing them with new ones is a tough endeavor. You will fail. Everyone does. After you review the reasons for your failure, let it go. Don't beat yourself up over it.

I've lost count of the number of times I tried, and failed, to implement an exercise routine. Likewise, I failed dozens of times to give up ice cream before finally succeeding.

The point is to give yourself a break. Remember, developing good habits is a marathon, not a sprint.

There's no better time than now to start making positive changes that will boost your productivity. Start planning how you'll address each habit listed in this action guide. By this time next year, you could be getting things done more quickly and effectively, and living a more rewarding life as a result.

May I Ask You A Small Favor?

The success of any book is dependent on readers' reviews. In other words, you control whether others find and benefit from this action guide.

If you enjoyed *The 30-Day Productivity Plan*, please let me know by leaving a quick review at Amazon.com. Writing a review only takes a few moments. And you'll be helping me and other readers in the process.

One last note: I'm grateful you've allowed me to spend time with you in this action guide. I realize the time you and I spent together could have been spent elsewhere. So thank you.

 Additionally, I want to congratulate you. Devoting yourself to habit change takes commitment and grit. You obviously have both as you've reached the end of this guide.

I'd like to welcome you to join my mailing list and claim your free gift at the following link:

http://artofproductivity.com/free-gift/

It's my hope that you and I will continue to work together in boosting your productivity and creating a more rewarding life!

Talk to you soon,
Damon Zahariades

About The Author

Damon Zahariades is a corporate refugee who endured years of unnecessary meetings, drive-by chats with coworkers and a distraction-laden work environment before striking out on his own. Today, in addition to being the author of a growing catalog of time management and productivity books, he's the showrunner for the productivity blog ArtofProductivity.com.

In his spare time, he shows off his copywriting chops by powering the content marketing campaigns used by today's growing businesses to attract customers.

Damon lives in Southern California with his beautiful, supportive wife and their frisky dog. He's currently staring down the barrel of his 50th birthday.

Other Productivity Action Guides by Damon Zahariades

Small Habits Revolution: 10 Steps To Transforming Your Life Through The Power Of Mini Habits!

Do you have 5 minutes a day to improve your life? Adopting good habits is tough. Maintaining them is even tougher. *Small Habits Revolution* describes an unconventional, highly-effective system for forming habits that stick.

* * *

To-Do List Formula: A Stress-Free Guide To Creating To-Do Lists That Work!

Most people use to-do lists that hamper their productivity and leave them with unfinished tasks. This action guide highlights the reasons and shows you how to create effective to-do lists that guarantee you get your important work done!

* * *

The Time Chunking Method: A 10-Step Action Plan For Increasing Your Productivity

The Time Chunking Method is one of the most popular time management strategies in use today. If you struggle with getting things done, you need this action guide. Productivity experts around the world attest to the method's effectiveness!

***

The 30-Day Productivity Plan: Break The 30 Bad Habits That Are Sabotaging Your Time Management - One Day At A Time!

This action guide will help you to identify and break the bad habits that are preventing you from achieving your goals. Organized into 30 easy-to-read daily chapters, it's filled with hundreds of actionable tips.

***

Digital Detox: Unplug To Reclaim Your Life

Stress levels are rising. Relationships are suffering. Our phones and other devices are largely to blame. *Digital Detox* provides a step-by-step blueprint for people who want to take a break from technology and enjoy life unplugged.

For a complete list, please visit
http://artofproductivity.com/my-books/

Made in the USA
Columbia, SC
27 July 2018